Australian Wine Walkabout

Also by David Copp

Hungary: Its Fine Wines and Winemakers

Tokaj: For the Bibulous Traveller

Bordeaux St Estephe

n

ut

ustralian

First p

ISBN

Copyrig

The right of David Copp

has been asserted by

Design

CONTENTS

INTRODUCTION

Australian Wine Walkabout is written from notes taken during several visits to Australia combined with those taken at tastings of Australian wines in the UK. It is not intended as a comprehensive guide to Australian wines, but simply an introduction in notebook form to some of her leading winemakers.

Having been trained in the classic wine regions of Europe I was ignorant about Australian wines until my employers took on the UK Agency for Michelton Wines in the 1970s.

About the same time, my good friend Paul Bouchard, the Burgundian shipper who frequently travelled Down Under to sell his wines, strongly recommended that I visit Australia because 'their growers have a refreshing and innovative approach to viticulture which will make a telling difference to the quality of their wines'. Some of the viticulturalists and winemakers he mentioned included Richard Smart, Brian Croser, Tony Jordan and Andrew Pirie.

I first visited Victoria and New South Wales in 1983, returning in the 1990s, and again with the Circle of Wine Writers in 2008 when we also covered South Australia and Tasmania. Bouchard's prediction has been proven accurate in that Australian fine wines have developed significantly due to the advances made by her leading viticulturalists and the vision, energy and skills of her winemakers.

There are more than 2300 independent Australian winemakers but my notes are restricted to those 150 or so that I have visited, met or whose wines I have tasted. My biggest hope is that these notes might encourage fellow wine enthusiasts to make their own voyages of discovery Down Under and find many others.

A SHORT HISTORY

The first vines to arrive in Australia came with Captain Arthur Philip, the newly appointed Governor-General of New South Wales in 1788. They came from the Cape of Good Hope but did not thrive in the humid climate close to the ocean. In fact it took a great deal of expertise and perseverance to get the Australian wine industry under way and the first commercial wines were not produced until the 1820s.

Further progress owed a great deal to the zeal of James Busby, a gifted Scots botanist who, recognizing the potential for vines in Australia, returned to Europe, and according to the wine historian HE Laffer, selected 678 vinifera vine cuttings from various European vineyards, which he brought back to propagate in New South Wales in the 1830s. Busby also found the time to write a practical guide for such aspiring vintners as the Doctors Lindeman and Penfold. It was entitled *A Manual of Plain Directions for Planting and Cultivating Vineyards and Making Wine in New South Wales.*

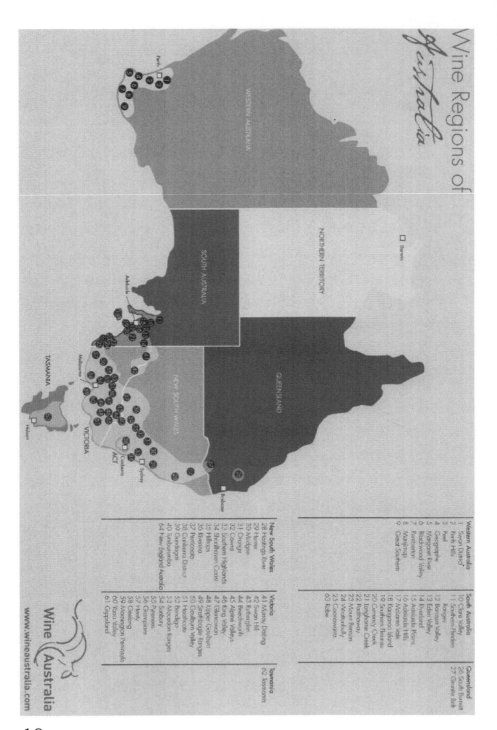

Wine Regions of Australia

Western Australia	South Australia	Queensland
1 Swan District	10 Clare Valley	26 South Burnett
2 Perth Hills	11 Southern Flinders	27 Granite Belt
3 Peel	Ranges	
4 Geographe	12 Barossa Valley	
5 Margaret River	13 Eden Valley	
6 Blackwood Valley	14 Riverland	
7 Pemberton	15 Adelaide Plains	
8 Manjimup	16 Adelaide Hills	
9 Great Southern	17 McLaren Vale	
	18 Kangaroo Island	
	19 Southern Fleurieu	
	20 Currency Creek	
	21 Langhorne Creek	
	22 Padthaway	
	23 Mount Benson	
	24 Wrattonbully	
	25 Coonawarra	
	65 Robe	

New South Wales	Victoria	Tasmania
28 Hastings River	41 Murray Darling	62 Tasmania
29 Hunter	42 Swan Hill	
30 Mudgee	43 Rutherglen	
31 Orange	44 Beechworth	
32 Cowra	45 Alpine Valleys	
33 Southern Highlands	46 King Valley	
34 Shoalhaven Coast	47 Glenrowan	
35 Hilltops	48 Upper Goulburn	
36 Riverina	49 Strathbogie Ranges	
37 Perricoota	50 Goulburn Valley	
38 Canberra District	51 Heathcote	
39 Gundagai	52 Bendigo	
40 Tumbarumba	53 Macedon Ranges	
64 New England Australia	54 Sunbury	
	55 Pyrenees	
	56 Grampians	
	57 Henty	
	58 Geelong	
	59 Mornington Peninsula	
	60 Yarra Valley	
	61 Gippsland	

The establishment of the free Colony of South Australia in 1836 attracted hundreds of British and German immigrants some of whom also helped to put the wine industry on a firmer footing. Dr Christopher Penfold and his wife Mary, from Brighton in England, planted vines at their Magill estate near Adelaide in the 1840s while John Riddoch, a fruit-farming Scot, pioneered Coonawarra. Samuel Smith, a Dorset brewer, settled in the Barossa Valley and Thomas Hardy, a Devonshire farmer's son, started in McLaren Vale. Another Scot, Dr John Ferguson, took over the Houghton vineyards in Western Australia. The 1850s Gold Rush in Victoria led to heavy plantings in the north east of the State in a game attempt to slake the thirst of the 40,000 prospectors who came from all over the world, hoping to make their fortune.

About the same time George Angas, a wealthy investor in South Australia, brought around 500 Silesian Lutheran farming families to the Barossa Valley. They tried to grow all kinds of crops and found that vines grew well. Thus, in the second half of the nineteenth century the Australian wine industry got under way and developed steadily until the wretched root aphid phylloxera devastated the Victorian vineyards from 1875-85. In the first half of the twentieth century two World Wars separated by an economic recession did little to revive the table wine trade which remained dominated by the demand for inexpensive fortified wines.

The rise of table wine

Ironically, Penfolds interest in increasing its fortified wine trade led to the revival of table wines. In 1950 the company sent its Chief Winemaker Max Schubert to Europe to learn about Sherry and Port production techniques. Having completed his studies in Jerez and Oporto, Schubert took the opportunity to visit Bordeaux where he was introduced to its great red wines. He was so impressed with the concentration, complexity and longevity of the wines he tasted that he determined to try and emulate them in Australia.

He produced his first Grange Hermitage in 1951. Grange was the name of Dr Penfold's surgery and Hermitage, the word commonly used for the Shiraz grape from the Rhone. Schubert's colleagues, who had little experience of tasting concentrated freshly fermented new wine maturing in new French oak barrels, were not impressed with his efforts. Fortunately for Australia, Schubert persevered and Penfolds Grange, as it is now called, is sold in Bordeaux alongside the very classified growths that Schubert had sought to emulate. He proved that Australia could produce complex, long lasting table wines of the highest quality.

Penfolds was not the only company trying to produce fine wine. Several other family owned companies were similarly engaged. In the Hunter Valley McWilliams, which had taken over Maurice O'Shea's vineyard at Mount Pleasant, continued to make top quality Semillons. Murray Tyrell 'acquired' some cuttings of the original Busby Chardonnay vines to produce the first commercial varietal wine. In Coonawarra David Wynn made fine Cabernet Sauvignon and Shiraz, while in Western Australia three wine loving doctors - Cullity, Cullen and Pannell - made highly promising Chardonnays in the area around Margaret River.

Soon afterwards two visionary young winemakers, Brian Croser and Dr Andrew Pirie PhD, found cooler vineyard sites in the

Adelaide Hills and Tasmania respectively, where they produced such European classic varieties as Chardonnay, Pinot Noir, Riesling and Sauvignon Blanc. In the Yarra Valley, a wine loving botanist named Bailey Carrodus began producing very fine Chardonnay and Cabernet Sauvignon.

The dynamics that set the scene for Brand Australia

World demand for Chardonnay and Cabernet Sauvignon in the late 1980s and 1990s was so great that several Australian companies invested in vast new plantings of popular varieties in the heartlands of New South Wales, South Australia and Victoria.

Highly efficient production, sales and marketing of remarkably well made, fruit driven table wines helped Australian wine exports to soar.

In the meantime, the South Australian Government decided to replace old plantings of Shiraz in the Barossa Valley (used for making port-style fortified wines) with new plantings of the more fashionable French varieties. Their approach was logical enough but it incensed

14

Barossa vintners such as Peter Lehmann who loved old vine Shiraz. Lehmann inspired fellow vintners to rescue as many of the older vines as possible and then show the world just what complex and enduring wines they made.

Thus between 1950 and 1985 the shape of Australia's future table wine production was established with wide scale planting of European varieties in South East Australia and the preservation of old vine Shiraz (and Grenache) in the Barossa Valley.

Increasing the awareness of Australian table wines

The 1956 Melbourne Olympics increased world wide awareness of Australia, and visitor numbers rose dramatically with the introduction of Boeing 707 passenger jet services in 1962, and the opening of the iconic Sydney Opera House in 1973.

The success of Australian sportsmen in international competition also contributed to the image of Australia as a young, dynamic country with a 'will-to-win' attitude, epitomized by Australia's victory in the 1983 Americas Cup yacht races. The worldwide success of the

Australian comedy film *Crocodile Dundee* was also used to promote Australian table wines.

During this period other significant developments encouraged table wine sales. Legislation was introduced to end the 'six o'clock swill' – the hour after work when bars were licensed to sell alcohol – and to extend licensing hours for hotels, restaurants and clubs where table wine consumption was greatest.

The Australian invention of the bag-in-a-box container made wine more affordable for younger Australians, and opened up the market to new consumers. Previously, table wine consumption had largely been confined to French imports served in the better hotels, restaurants and clubs of Melbourne and Sydney.

The role of the Australian Wine and Brandy Corporation (AWBC)

AWBC selected a perky Welsh immigrant named Len Evans as their first wine promotions manager, and he proved to be an absolute star. He became an accomplished communicator, wine writer and educator, gifted taster, Wine Show judge and great ambassador for Australian wine around the world. His greatest achievement was encouraging Australians to drink their own table wines.

As a result of the surge in table wine consumption international marketers such as Philip Morris, HJ Heinz, Reckitt & Colman and Tooheys Breweries invested in the wine industry and the Government granted tax incentives to encourage further planting.

The producers marketing strategy was sensibly straightforward: prompt delivery of well-produced popular varieties, simply labelled, attractively packaged, and constantly promoted as good value-for-money wines. In the twenty years between 1985 and 2005 Australian table wine exports rose from practically nothing to A$ 6.5 billion, making Australia the world's fourth largest wine exporter, with brands that dominated the wine shelves of the world's largest retailers.

In 1996 AWBC published a 30 year plan to ensure continuity of its thrust into world markets. However, within ten years most of the key objectives had been achieved, and a revised plan was required.

The revised plan of 2007 took into account the fact that the industry's production and sales dynamics were changing dramatically. World production of wine exceeded consumption and competition amongst producer countries had driven down prices in real terms. At the same time, rationalization of the retail trade had squeezed producer margins. Moreover, severe water usage restrictions were imposed in the three largest Australian wine-producing regions of Riverland, Murray Darling Basin and Riverina where crop irrigation is essential for high yield production. Matters were made worse by adverse foreign exchange rates which increased costs to consumers in key markets and the 2007 world economic recession.

Furthermore, Australia's phenomenal export success had prompted reaction from competitor producer countries. The so-called Old World wine producers (France, Italy and Spain), stung by their loss of market share, began to fight back. At the same time, other New World producers such as South Africa, Chile and Argentine, whose exports had hitherto been restricted by economic sanctions, were now free to trade, and directed their efforts at the very trade sectors in which Australia had been so successful.

Realising that Australia would no longer be able to compete on price terms with competitive producer countries, AWBC amended its strategy to give greater marketing emphasis to the development of its premium wine trade. Fortunately, a number of independent regional vintners had followed Penfolds path, underlining the fact that Australia could produce a diverse range of quality wines similar to that of the French wine regions.

The revised marketing strategy is to support successfully established brands such as Jacobs Creek and Hardy with premium quality wines from regional growers such as those in the Adelaide Hills, Clare Valley, Eden Valley, McLaren Vale, Barossa Valley and Coonawarra in South Australia: the Hunter Valley in New South Wales: Yarra Valley, Mornington Peninsula and Goulburn Valley in Victoria: Margaret River in Western Australia and Tasmania.

This radical change in plan will take time, patience and collective effort to implement and supposes that the industry will work together towards its new goals. There is bound to be tension between larger public companies with shareholders to satisfy, and smaller family enterprises with different imperatives, particularly when it comes to spending scarce promotional dollars to reshape public perceptions of Australian wine.

In short, this is a difficult period for the Australian wine industry but there are several positive factors that should be kept top of mind. Firstly, Australia has proved that she can produce a diverse range of distinctive, world class wines. Secondly, Australians are resilient people with a 'can-do' approach to life which made them the world's fourth largest exporter of wines. Thirdly, Australia is closer to the promising Asian markets than many of her main competitors. As the balance of world trade shifts to the east, where two thirds of the world's population now live, there is a vast new market to exploit. That market includes many people living in tropical climates close to sources of fresh seafood, and many Chinese who are red wine enthusiasts. It seems that Australia's refreshing cool climate whites and her unique Shiraz have good prospects.

Australian Viticulture

In the brief review of the history of Australian wine we saw how early botanists and pioneers worked hard to establish the vine in Australia. Their work has been continued by a stream of highly qualified modern viticulturalists who have contributed to the improvement of plantations. They have not only learned from their own scientific institutions but have broadened their experience by working in other wine producing countries.

Australian viticulturalists are generally more flexible than their European counterparts because they are less hidebound by tradition, more open to new ideas and practices, and because as large-scale producers of popular wines, they needed to be able to respond quickly to market signals which have indicated changes in consumer's wine style preferences.

They are also more pragmatic. Whereas European vignerons (who are both growers and winemakers) are driven by tradition and a sense of place, the larger scale Australian producers see themselves as processors of farmed grapes which, thanks to refrigerated transport, can be trucked to an appropriate processing centre where the prime task is to extract fruit flavour rather than the characteristics of the terrain.

They are also pragmatic in their approach to mechanisation of such routine vineyard work such as ploughing, vine canopy management and harvesting. Because Australia is one of the world's warmest wine-producing countries, and labour is relatively scarce and expensive, they have designed operationally efficient mechanised equipment to do maintenance work and gather grapes quickly when they reach optimum ripeness.

The same pragmatic approach has been applied to irrigation. Australia is the world's driest continent and most of its vineyards require some sort of irrigation, so efficient drip irrigation techniques were needed. However, as water becomes increasingly scarce and expensive, growers are turning to other means of producing healthy grapes. Some have reverted to dry-farming techniques, others have moved to cooler sites, while others have taken to planting drought resistant varieties. For the longer term, genetic modification of vines may provide an answer.

Australian Wine Research Institute

The industry has been extremely well served by the Australian Wine Research Institute (AWRI) which has an excellent record for publishing world class technical and scientific papers on a wide range of subjects including the relationship between grape chemistry and wine flavour, identifying volatile compounds in wine, the role of oxygen in wine, canopy management, closure trials and post bottling wine chemistry.

Funded by grape growers and producers and the Federal Government, which matches the contribution of the growers and producers, its current research projects include the effects of global warming and water usage in winemaking, and the genetic modification of yeasts and grapevines.

AWRI also provides practical help to its members in dealing with such diverse problems as removing smoke taint from wines, managing minty (eucalyptus) flavours in red wines and dealing with stuck fermentations at harvest time.

It was a pleasure to meet the AWRI managing director Professor Isak (Sakkie)

Pretroius who has led this research team so well and who organized an extremely useful fault finding course for us during our visit.

Summary

My most recent visit to Australia has reinforced my conviction that Australia has a strong body of outstanding grape growers and highly qualified, intuitive winemakers producing world class wines. I found those that I met more positive about terroir, less reliant on technology, and more interested in developing varietal or regional expression.

I also noted that there are more vineyards in higher, cooler sites, more densely planted with better clonal material, and more appropriately matched to soil and climate. There is even greater precision in vineyard work resulting in lower yields of riper, healthier grapes which produce more complex, distinctive and longer lived wines.

My own view is that that it is probably best for the Australian wine industry to bite the bullet now and develop a sustainable premium wine trade without further delay.

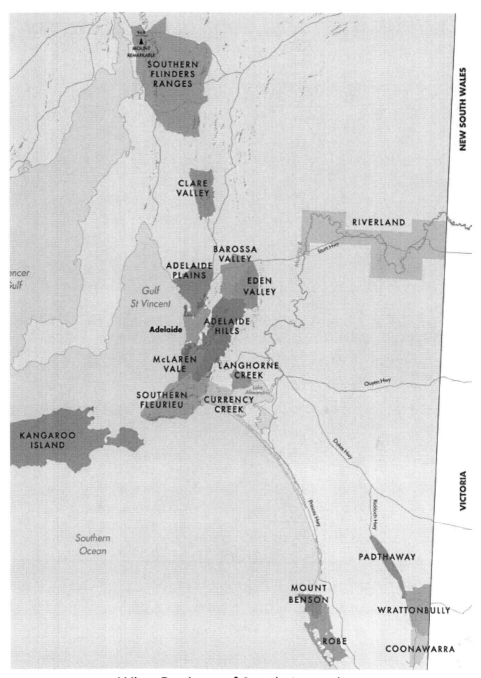

Wine Regions of South Australia

ADELAIDE HILLS

A delaide, the State capital of South Australia established in 1836, was built on a one mile square site completely surrounded by parkland.

Often referred to as the 'twenty minute city' because one can walk from one end of it to the other in that time, Adelaide is set out on a grid system with its splendid main boulevards interspaced with large squares that show off both its original architecture and sensitively designed modern buildings.

Europeans were first attracted by the new State's commitment to civil liberty and religious tolerance but many more settlers subsequently came to start a new life in the aftermath of the two World Wars. Today people come in search of work in such modern industries as defence technology, electronics, motor manufacture and wine. South Australia produces half Australia's wine and Adelaide is the centre of the Australian wine industry.

Adelaide Hills, arguably one of the most attractive of Australia's many wine regions, is a mere 30 minute drive east of the city. There are splendid views of the city from the summit of the 720 metre high Mount Lofty from where the Gulf of St Vincent can be seen to the west, and the vineyards of the Piccadilly Valley to the east.

Piccadilly and Lenswood (pictured above) are the two sub-regions of Adelaide Hills. Both lie in the lee of the mountain, have an annual rainfall in the 700-900mm range, and enjoy mainly dry sunny, summers refreshed by sea breezes blowing off the Great Australian Bight. Since the Adelaide Hills is a crucial catchment area for Adelaide's water supply, water usage is strictly regulated and the number of wineries limited, encouraging producers to focus on quality rather than quantity.

The best vineyards are found on sun facing slopes 400-650 metres above sea level. At this altitude average daytime temperatures are 4C cooler than at sea level. Warm, dry summers with cool nights are ideal conditions in which to grow grapes with good fruit composition, natural acidity and a wide spectrum of flavour.

The grey-brown loam soils were first planted with vines in the 1840's but when the fashion turned to fortified wines, unwanted vineyards were abandoned. The renaissance of table wine production in the region was largely due to the determination of Brian Croser to find an Australian site on which to grow Chardonnay with the same levels of acidity and fruit flavour obtained in Burgundy. In 1976 he found the ideal site in the Piccadilly valley and formed the Petaluma Company. His success encouraged other growers to move into the Hills and the appellation now covers 3,700 hectares mostly planted to Chardonnay, Sauvignon Blanc, Pinot Noir and Shiraz.

The coolness of the higher Piccadilly slopes helped Petaluma produce excellent sparkling wine, good enough to win the admiration of Champagne Bollinger which invested in the company.

Adelaide Hills is recognised for the excellence of its Sauvignon Blanc, a variety that became immensely popular after New Zealand's Cloudy Bay burst into the market in 1985. At first Adelaide Hills winemakers tried to emulate the Kiwi style but soon realised that they could make crisp, subtle, less herbaceous Sauvignon Blanc of their own. They have since enjoyed greater success with the variety.

More recently the Adelaide Hills have attracted many Pinot Noir enthusiasts. Tim Knappstein of Lenswood Vineyards sold his original Clare Valley company to concentrate on producing Pinot Noir here. Stephen George of Ashton Mills is another Pinot Noir specialist, Penfolds and Jeffrey Grosset all source their Pinot Noir from the region.

SHAW + SMITH

Michael Hill Smith MW and his cousins Martin and Matthew Shaw established their winery in 1989, having carefully selected a 42 hectare site at Woodside to produce premium quality Sauvignon Blanc and Chardonnay. They later acquired another 36 hectare site at nearby

Balhannah to produce Shiraz, Pinot Noir, Sauvignon Blanc and Riesling.

The free-draining sandy loam at Woodside suits Sauvignon Blanc. The vines are pruned to an arched cane system which gives leaves and grapes better exposure to the sun and helps control excessive vine vigour. Michael Hill Smith assembled six fresh and fruity Sauvignon Blancs from different regional producers all of which demonstrated that thinner soils and effective canopy management produce clean, crisp, elegant wines with excellent varietal expression.

The flight of six regional Chardonnays (mostly 2007s) that followed showed the variety at its best, expressing the nuances of the different terroirs. The climate allows Chardonnay to develop its fruit character. Shaw + Smith's M3 Chardonnay is rich and creamy: Tapanappa's Tiers Vineyard has mineral edge: the most polished wine (benefitting from an extra 12 months of ageing) was the beautifully balanced, full bodied, barrel fermented Penfolds 2006 Bin 60 A. The common denominator in all six wines was purity of fruit flavour, depth and complexity developed by sensitive growing and handling, and the length of the wines.

Pinot Noir production is now well into its stride with the help of improved Dijon clonal material. The Smith + Shaw version shows pure and subtle fruit flavours which will surely develop as the relatively young vines come to maturity. Tim Knappstein's Lenswood and Stephen George's Ashton Mills also exhibit the excellence that can be achieved from this variety in the Adelaide Hills.

Prompted by Penfold's senior winemaker John Davoren, Adelaide Hills growers have begun to produce cool climate Shiraz around Mount Barker, and this lighter, richer, more elegant style of Shiraz is becoming increasingly popular. The Shaw + Smith Shiraz made at Balhannah showed spicy black fruit and smooth tannins: it was an elegant and charming wine.

Woodside is an extremely attractive and well run winery. Its modern design and cool interior décor provide a relaxed atmosphere in which to taste wines.

The founders and principal partners are mature winemakers, constantly fine-tuning their skills as they develop their well balanced portfolio of premium wines. Michael Hill Smith MW is not complacent. He knows that the more they learn about their soils, climate and clonal material, the better the wines will be.

THE LANE

John, Helen and Marty Edwards used to grow grapes for Constellation Wines but now have their own boutique winery at Ravenswood Lane near Hahndorf in the heart of the picturesque Adelaide Hills.

Their 52 hectares are planted to nine different varieties including Chardonnay, Sauvignon Blanc and Shiraz, varieties well matched to the variable soil, aspect, and climatic conditions of the undulating hills. The very, very old soils with limestone/calcareous content ensure vibrant acidity in the wines.

John's background in the diamond industry has shaped his direct approach to life and plain speaking. 'Our aim is to bring the vineyard into the glass with as little interference as possible,' he says as he whisks us through the winery, sampling the 2008's that were still in tank. 'The better we look after our vines, the less work we have to do in the winery,' he summarises succinctly.

The winery restaurant is billed as a bistro but all the food is locally sourced, beautifully prepared and paired with the wines. The Sauvignon Blanc/Semillon blend, appropriately named The Gathering, was a crisp and flavoursome accompaniment to the mature goats' cheese; two elegant Chardonnays accompanied the fish course while a mature and well rounded 2003 Shiraz blend, The Lane Reunion, was well suited to succulent lamb chops.

The Edwards concentrate on developing the fruit flavour of their wines. The winemaking has an admirably light touch, producing stylish modern wines for discerning drinkers. The Lane has a refreshing approach to making fine premium wines and it was good to see its busy restaurant so well used by locals obviously enjoying themselves.

PETALUMA

Petaluma, founded by Brian Croser in 1976, to produce premium quality wines with a difference, became so successful that it was the subject of a hostile take-over bid from diversifying brewer Lion Nathan in 2001.

The new owners persuaded Croser to stay on for three years to ensure continuity of the Petaluma brand and to hand over to his successor, Andrew Hardy. The new team is committed to Croser's original concept as we found when we tasted their portfolio of wines, as well as samples from such other leading local producers as Chain of Ponds, Nepenthe and Geoff Weaver.

It was a nice touch to start the tasting with mature Croser sparkling wines made from estate grown Chardonnay (37%) and Pinot Noir (63%). The elegant, polished, richly flavoured wines that so impressed the Bollinger family are in good shape.

Ripening conditions for Chardonnay and Pinot Noir in the Piccadilly Valley are superb: warm days and cool nights combine to develop fruit flavours and tannins. Croser selected the latest Dijon clones, planted them at higher than normal density (for Australia) and introduced precise viticultural practices to deliver top quality fruit.

The Petaluma Chardonnay varietal wines (Petaluma Tiers and Piccadilly Valley) are full flavoured but subtle and intriguing. The winery does not produce a Pinot Noir varietal but showed us two competitor wines – a superb 1999 Ashton Hills that won the Adelaide Hills 'Wine of the Show' award, and Tim Knappstein's 2003 Pinot Noir, voted 'Best Pinot Noir in Southern Australia.' We also tasted a very promising locally produced Nebbiolo, the Italian variety that has been described as 'Pinot Noir with attitude' because it is more site specific and temperamental than its cousin.

BRIAN CROSER

A South Australian farmer's son born in 1949 Brian Croser is a visionary winemaker in the mould of Maurice O'Shea and Max Schubert, and his contemporary Dr Andrew Pirie. His uncompromising approach to every aspect of viticulture and winemaking has earned him respect and made him one of the most outstanding antipodean winemakers. Voted Decanter's Man of the Year in 2004 he stayed

over in London after the awards ceremony to facilitate a tasting for the Circle of Wine Writers, offering us a memorable glimpse of the shape of things to come with samples of his sparkling wine, Clare Valley Riesling, Tiers Chardonnay, Viognier and Shiraz from Mount Barker, and Coonawarra Cabernets.

Having studied viticulture in South Australia and at the University of California Davis (UCD) Croser started his career as a winemaker with Hardy's, before leaving in 1976 to found Petaluma. In 1977 he led the first Wine Science Course at what is now Charles Sturt University and in 1978 formed Oenotec, an oenological consultancy, with Dr Tony Jordan.

From the start of his career Brian Croser differed from many of his Australian contemporaries in that he espoused the European concept of terroir. He set out to scour Australia for what he called 'distinguished' sites suitable for those classic European varieties -Chardonnay and Riesling, Cabernet Sauvignon, Pinot Noir and Syrah-in which he was most interested. His first such find was in the Piccadilly Valley which he named the Tiers vineyard. It was planted to Chardonnay in the coolest part, and to Pinot Noir in the warmest. He later found, or was steered to, other 'distinguished' sites such as those around Mount Barker in the Adelaide Hills, at Hanlin Hill in the Clare Valley, in the friable soils around Wrattonbully just to the north of Coonawarra and, more recently, in the

Fleurieu Peninsula south of Adelaide where he has planted Pinot Noir.

Croser brought a revolutionary approach to Australian viticulture, planting at higher than normal (Australian) density, pruning and training his vines to achieve a better balance in leaf and fruit growth. In the winery, his knowledge of plant physiology and the chemical and physical properties of grapes allowed him to develop techniques that were beyond the compass of the average Australian winemaker preoccupied with making basic wines fortified with alcohol. His winemaking mantra remains the preservation and enhancement of the natural fruit flavours of a particular grape variety planted in a particular site.

In order to develop his concept on a wider scale in the Clare Valley, Mornington Peninsula, Goulburn Valley and Western Australia, Croser sought public subscription and in so doing opened himself up to corporate raiders. One such was the Lion Nathan brewing group which, in 2001, succeeded in a hostile bid for Petaluma.

Croser was disconsolate at losing control of the company he had created. The new owners tried to mitigate the blow by retaining his services for three years to maintain the integrity of the brand he had created and bring on his successors. Thus it was not until 2004 that he started the third phase of his career, developing his original concept in partnership with the Bollinger family and the Medocain producer, Jean Michel Cases of Chateau Lynch Bages. The Tiers vineyard in Piccadilly, always a Croser family property, was the basis of the new Tapanappa company.

With his new partners he acquired sites at Wrattonbully on the Limestone Coast and on the Fleurieu Peninsula, south of McLaren Vale. The first fruits of his new labours of love reveal rich promise. He remains an out and out terroirist, delighting in making wines that express the qualities and the character of the sites he has so carefully chosen to develop.

Croser's vision and proven ability makes him worth following wherever he goes. He has been involved in projects in Oregon and Chile (with Santa Rita) and keeps a close eye on fine winemaking developments in other world regions. However, his heart is closest to the true personality of Australian wine regions which, together with an increasing number of outstanding Australian wine makers, he is determined to bring to wider attention.

AUSTRALIAN CHARDONNAY

It is sobering to recall that when I first visited Australia in 1983 hardly any Chardonnay was grown at all. And yet 27 years later it is the second most widely planted variety in Australia. Chardonnay became so popular in the 1980s that it became a generic term for white wine – and several new mothers named their baby daughters after it. In the 1990s it was extensively planted throughout Australia and production rose from 11,000 tonnes in 1985 to 252,000 in 2005.

Wine enthusiasts have appreciated the buttery richness of fine Burgundy for centuries without realizing it was made from Chardonnay. However, the success of Californian Chardonnay at the so-called Judgment of Paris Tasting in 1976, brought the variety into the spotlight and showed that good Chardonnay could also be produced outside the Cote d'Or. Australian vintners determined to show that they too could produce quality wines from this classic variety.

Chardonnay is popular with growers because it takes easily to calcareous soils, ripens early and is a sound and reliable cropper producing richly flavoured wines. Moreover, it is a very malleable variety that lends itself to different styles of winemaking, reductive or oxidative: on the skins or off them: with malolactic fermentation or without: and is responsive to different levels of oak treatment.

It is also a variety that reflects the personality of its terroir. In Chablis it is often described as 'flinty', in Meursault 'rich', in Puligny and in Chassagne Montrachet, 'concentrated' and 'powerful.' In California, (where the wines are mostly matured in American wood) toasty, while in Australia, very ripe Chardonnay fruit, tempered with new oak, led Wine Show judges to enthuse about its 'rich mouth feel'.

The first Chardonnay vines in Australia were planted in the Hunter Valley by James Busby in 1832 and it was from their descendants on the Penfolds estate that the Hunter Valley grower Murray Tyrell (by his own admission) 'borrowed' some cuttings to see how they would do. In 1971 he produced his first commercial Chardonnay which was considered a great success, and the variety has flourished ever since.

Another early pioneer in the Hunter Valley was Dr Max Lake, a surgeon and wine enthusiast who produced Chardonnay to a high standard (that has been maintained by his successor Rod Kempe) at Lakes Folly.

In South Australia Brian Croser found a great site for Chardonnay in the in the Piccadilly Valley as did David Wynn in the Eden Valley: In Tasmania Dr Andrew Pirie, found ideal conditions in the Tamar Valley above Launceston and in Western Australia Doctors Cullitt, Cullen and Pannell followed the advice of Dr John Gladstones and established Chardonnay vineyards in Margaret River followed in 1982 by Denis Horgan, at Leeuwin Estate who was mentored by Robert Mondavi, one of the most successful Californian producers. 1982 was also the year in which mechanical engineer turned

winemaker Rick Kinzbrunner planted Chardonnay in his Giaconda vineyard near Beechworth, Victoria. Three years later James Halliday, corporate lawyer turned winemaker (pictured left) founded Coldstream Hills in

the Yarra Valley and made wine described by a good friend as the 'Australian Chardonnay most like Burgundy'. At the same time large quantities of basic Chardonnay were being planted in the irrigated areas of Upper Victoria, South Australia and New South Wales to meet the growing demand from large consumer markets such as UK and USA. By the mid-1990s Australia had established a world wide reputation for big, fruity Chardonnays and exports rocketed. As a result every other producer country turned to producing it in large quantities and, as so often happens when a particular variety becomes over-popular, quality suffers as competition to sell increases. Thus many Chardonnays were but poor shadows of the real thing. Twenty years after mothers first named their baby daughters Chardonnay, the name became a term of abuse so much so that an AbC (Anything but Chardonnay) group of wine drinkers formed.

Australian growers, realizing that public preferences had changed to fruity but less alcoholic, less heavily oaked wines, adapted vinifications accordingly. At the same time top quality producers such as Croser, Halliday, Pirie and Leeuwin were earning recognition for the elegance and finesse of their Chardonnays made in the European style, yet with a positive Australian personality. Having sampled Chardonnays from all the main Australian wine regions I am convinced that she offers a wider choice of styles than any other producer country including France.

As we have seen the first commercial Chardonnay was produced in the Lower Hunter but growers have since acknowledged that Chardonnay performs better in cooler sites higher up the Valley. Clones of James Busby's original Chardonnay plantings have been found in Mudgee where creamy, peachy wines are the order of the day. Chardonnay also dominates the plantings in Orange in the Central Highlands, producing fleshy and fruity wines. Even higher in the Snowy Mountains at 842 metres above sea level, McWilliams produces Banwang 842 Chardonnay with a memorably flinty nose, savoury flavours, and a long, persistent mineral finish.

The Margaret River Chardonnays are voluptuous, concentrated and complex, subtle and sophisticated. Leeuwin, Cullen, Voyager Estate, Pierro, Vasse Felix, Evans & Tate, McHenry Hohnen, Xanadu are just some of the impressive wines I have tasted. Cullen's Kevin John Chardonnay 2007 was named as 'Best Chardonnay' in the 2010 Decanter Awards. Decanter has one of the most qualified and demanding of all competition judging panels.

The South Australian Chardonnays from Adelaide Hills and Eden Valley have a different character. Penfolds Yattarna – often referred to as the 'White Grange' – has all the qualities of the worlds best Chardonnays, produced from top quality fruit and sustained by vibrant acidity and beautiful balance. Brian Croser's Tiers Chardonnay and Shaw + Smith's M3 are outstanding examples from the Adelaide Hills. In the Eden valley Mountadam and Heggies lead the way with Eileen Hardy Chardonnay, which includes some Tasmanian fruit.

The best Tasmanian Chardonnays are no less impressive, if perhaps a little more austere. The importance of the Tasmanian sparkling wine trade means that growers naturally focus on the acid structure of the grapes they produce because it underpins the freshness of flavour and longevity that they seek for their fizz. They use wild yeasts for their varietal Chardonnays, and the lees are stirred during barrel-ageing to develop texture.

Andrew Pirie's Tasmanian Chardonnay is a classic of the kind.

Victoria produces a quarter of all Australian Chardonnay with flavours that range from the rich, weighty, white-stone fruit wines of Upper Goulburn through the highly aromatic, citrus flavoured Beechworth wines to the stunning and sophisticated Yarra Valley and Mornington Peninsula Chardonnays.

Over the last five or ten years the quality of the best Australian Chardonnays has changed more dramatically than any other major variety. There is no doubt that finding the right sites in cooler regions and improving the clonal selection of the vines is largely responsible for the improvement together with more precise viticulture. The grapes are harvested earlier to retain natural acids and maintain the balance between crispness and creamy, peachy flavours. Whole bunch pressing lees stirring and more gentle use of oak add more subtle flavours and greater elegance and finesse to the wine. Australia now produces some superb Chardonnay wines and it is good to see them being recognised by fine wine merchants around the world.

EDEN VALLEY

The Eden Valley is a sub-region of the Barossa Valley but I have included it in this section because it is essentially a cool climate white wine region although it also produces some of Australia's finest red wines.

The name suggests a lush green paradise through which tree-lined rivers flow timelessly,

but this Eden can have a rather lived-in appearance, due to the existence of old aboriginal dwelling sites, with blue-grey, silver and burnt brown colour tones as well as the bright green.

And yet from a viticultural point of view it is God's own country. The first vines were planted by an Englishman, Joseph Gilbert who proved to be an endearing character. Whilst reading *The Times* at home in Wiltshire, this 38 year old son of a well-to-do landowner saw an advertisement announcing the imminent departure of SS Buckinghamshire for the new colony of South Australia, and decided to take passage.

Having looked around the new colony he purchased 15,000 acres in the Barossa Ranges and planted a selection of different grape varieties on land that he named Pewsey Vale after his father's Wiltshire Estate. Having been satisfied that the newly planted vines had taken to their new surroundings Gilbert freely distributed cuttings to his neighbours, many of whom were hard-up Silesian immigrants.

The Eden Valley differs from Adelaide Hills in that it is cooler and drier and its topography more varied. It is a well balanced climate ideal for growing Riesling, Chardonnay, Viognier and Shiraz.

The highest sites are in the northern part of the valley where the ancient, acidic soils are planted to white varieties. At this height wind is a factor which restricts growth and thereby yield, yet enhances concentration of fruit flavours.

Leo Buring (1876-1961), the Australian born son of a German immigrant, was the first to produce classic Rieslings in the Eden valley and his successors John Vickery and Oliver Crawford have maintained his very high standards. Leo Buring Riesling is a genuine Australian classic, combining intense fruit flavours with wonderful freshness, purity, elegance and finesse, which matures gently over 10 years or more years.

Orlando Wyndham also created a new vineyard in rocky schist on the higher slopes. At first sight the land was declared 'good for nothing', but patience and understanding of the terroir have created Steingarten, a single vineyard Riesling that has become one of the most highly rated wines of the region.

Joseph Gilbert's original Pewsey Vale vineyards were purchased by Yalumba in 1961, renovated and expanded to produce Contours Riesling, another classic of the kind. Yalumba was so delighted with the quality of its Eden Valley Riesling that it created a new vineyard named Heggies (at 550 metres, one of the highest in the valley) where it produces a Reserve Riesling and a luscious botrytised Riesling with 20 g/l residual sugar, as well as its flagship Chardonnay produced from close-planted, low yielding Burgundian clones.

These leading producers are supported by a number of smaller family companies collectively known as the Twelve Apostles whose mission is to jointly promote Eden Valley Riesling. Each year they combine some of their very best fruit in a blend sold as Eden Valley Producers Riesling, a label you can buy with the utmost confidence. Mesh, a joint-venture project between two great winemakers – Robert Hill Smith and Jeffrey Grosset – is another classic Riesling with a growing following at home and abroad.

Apart from Riesling, Eden valley has several other strings to its bow. I have mentioned Yalumba's Heggies Chardonnay but the Eden valley is also home to Virgilius, one of Australia's finest Viogniers. The Yalumba winemaking team deserves enormous credit for their perseverance with this northern Rhone varietal which, at first, showed total indifference to its new home, refusing to be pushed around, making it quite clear to the viticulturalists that it would determine its own routine. Virgilius is a wonderful expression of Viognier: orange blossom and dried apricot flavours on the nose with flavours accentuated by the addition of a small quantity of botrytised fruit during the barrel fermentation. Brilliant winemaking, outstanding wine.

The topography changes in the southern end of the valley where red varieties are planted at 350-400 metres above sea level in grey-brown ironstone/gravel soils. It is here that we find Hill of Grace, one of Australia's best and most famous red wines. Before we visit the vineyard we should meet its owners, Stephen and Prue Henschke.

HENSCHKE

The Henschkes were Lutherans that came to the Barossa in the 1840s to escape a new Prussian regime intent on imposing Calvinism on its people. With other Silesian immigrants they were grateful for the chance to start a new life in religiously tolerant South Australia, and quickly settled to subsistence farming, planting vegetables, cereals, vines and fruit trees, and rearing cattle and livestock on the land they had been allocated.

The family grew grapes from the start and built a small winery. Five generations later, the winery and vineyards have been expanded to 60 hectares in the Eden Valley and a further 13 hectares in the Adelaide Hills but the firm remains a family enterprise, and is one of the most renowned in Australia for the quality of its wines.

In the early 1950s Cyril Henschke made two very significant decisions: to concentrate on table wine rather than fortified wine: and to make single vineyard wines rather than blends. His first single vineyard was labelled: *1952 Mount Edelstone Claret bottled by C A Henschke of the North Rhine Winery.* Although the wine was produced from Shiraz it was called 'claret' for the simple reason that wine labelled 'claret' sold better than wine labelled Shiraz. Wine Show judges admired it so much that they showered it with medals and awards and Cyril Henschke decided to produce another single vineyard wine. This time he selected the vineyard planted opposite the blue-stone Lutheran Church at Gnadenberg, which translates into English as Hill of Grace. The rest is history. Alongside Grange, Hill of Grace is the most revered red wine made in Australia. In Langtons Classification of Australian wines it is listed as Exceptional.

Just as Cyril Henschke had winemaking in his blood so does his son Stephen who graduated in bio-chemistry at Adelaide University before gaining work experience at  Rothbury Estate in the Hunter Valley and attending Geisenheim Wine Institute in Germany with his wife Prue, then a trainee viticulturalist. Having completed two years study in Germany the couple returned to Australia to enrol in the first ever Wine Science Course at Wagga Wagga, now Charles Sturt University.

During the holidays Stephen worked alongside his father while Prue trained as technical research officer at Roseworthy College working with Dr Richard Smart on various viticultural projects. When Stephen's father died prematurely the young-marrieds were well prepared to take over the family winery.

As one might expect from the family background, Henschke white wines owe more to German methods than Australian. The focus is on purity of fruit flavour through precise viticultural work. The range of white wines includes a pale gold, crisp Semillon, the intensely flavoured Julius Reserve Riesling, and the peach-nectarine aromas of Cranes Chardonnay.

The red wines are made in traditional style in open top fermenters to help soften the tannins. Johann's Garden is a smooth and subtle Grenache, Syrah, Mourvedre (GSM) blend; Mount Edelstone (the original claret now correctly labelled) is old vine Shiraz with

wonderfully subtle flavours. The Henschke cool climate Shiraz wines are less peppery than those from Adelaide Hills. Cabernet Sauvignon performs well in the lower Eden, and Cyril Henschke, a Cabernet-Merlot blend named for Stephen's father, is full bodied with luscious cassis-accented fruit flavours. Hill of Grace is the oldest and perhaps the best of all distinguished vineyard sites in Australia. Its 8 hectares include the 'Grandfather' plot of 1860 vines (shown above); others were planted in 1910. More recently Prue replanted a plot with cuttings from the sturdiest of the old vines. The wine from Hill of Grace vines is elegance personified. We tasted the 2004 and its blackberry and plum aromas and richly concentrated fruit are subtly presented with a gentleness that I found very appealing.

Every Henschke wine is distinctive and expressive of its variety. The same pursuit of excellence is evident. When I asked Stephen about his methods he modestly replied: 'We are fortunate to have inherited such superb terroirs and old vines which Prue nurses so carefully. It also helps that both of us were born with a natural spirit of enquiry, and we enjoy working together. Because purity of fruit flavour is important to us we set out to make sure that we properly understood whether it is derived from the soil, the climate or the grape. Our researches, and those of other oenologists, revealed the importance of photosynthesis (the process by which light energy is captured and converted to chemical energy in the form of glucose in the grape) and as a result, we have amended site-selection, canopy management and viticultural practices accordingly'. That seems to me to be the essence of Henschke.

The pilgrimage to the Hill of Grace vineyard is a profound experience. The 150 year old vines, with their branches trained upwards like hands raised in prayer, give the vineyard in front of the church, an air of reverence. The precious old vines are mulched with wheat straw to retain moisture and encourage microbial life. The grapes are handpicked and vinified block by block and when fermentation is well and truly under way the wine is run off into American oak because Stephen, like other leading Australian vintners, considers that the wine is better integrated with oak at an early stage. Henschke is one of the worlds truly great wineries, not for its size or output, but for the sheer love, affection and skill poured into every bottle by a remarkable man and wife team.

CLARE VALLEY

The Clare Valley, nearly 90 miles north of Adelaide, is the recognised Riesling capital of Australia. On arrival it was easy to appreciate why the early pioneers were so enthusiastic about Clare's three north-south elevated valleys, each lined with steep hills rising to 650 metres: each with slightly different soils.

Altitude is vital for the production of crisp, fragrant, fruit-flavoured Rieslings particularly if they are to have the natural acids that will give them freshness and long life.

Watervale and Polish Hill produce the best Rieslings: they are citrus fruit flavoured, juicy and excitingly mineral. They do not need oak. Clare's red wines are also very special. Small wineries like Wendouree, Grosset, Mitchells and Skillogalee produce stunning examples of Shiraz and Cabernet Sauvignon. However, we have come to the region to look at its Rieslings, about which a few words of introduction.

AUSTRALIAN RIESLING

If you are a Riesling enthusiast and you plan to visit Australia, make sure that you allocate at least two days to the Clare Valley, time enough to walk the 15 mile Riesling Trail which passes the cellar doors of several of the leading wineries. On the walk you will experience at first hand the climate and soils which are so perfect for growing this classic variety. The climatic conditions and soil are complemented by some of Australia's most skilful and dedicated winemakers.

My first understanding of the value of Riesling came with looking at English wine merchant lists from 100 years ago which revealed that the best Rhine and Mosel Rieslings were sold at higher prices than Bordeaux First Growths. Perhaps they are so special because they are made in quite difficult conditions at the northern extremes of wine producing Europe where vines demand dedicated viticulture. However, as we have seen with Chardonnay, popularity of a particular grape can be a two edged sword.

Riesling became so popular in post war Europe that greedy growers pushed yields up from 18hl/ha to 100 hl/ha. Worse still, they sugared their wines to such an extent that in England Riesling became a sickly shadow of the true original. Most of this sweet wine was labelled Liebfraumilch, a word that British wine drinkers came to despise. Riesling's name was equally abused in Australia where almost any dryish wine from Semillon, Colombard or Crouchen grapes was labelled Riesling on the grounds that it sold better. Thanks to the efforts of leading German growers Riesling's reputation has been restored, while in the Clare Valley, Riesling purists campaigned hard for its corrected labelling.

The best Rieslings, wherever they come from, are usually produced in cool climate areas on thin, mineral-rich, slatey soils from low yielding vines which encourage acidity and the development of fruit flavours. The main difference between Australian Rieslings and those of Germanic Europe is that the former have more body and pronounced citrus flavours while the latter show more delicate and I believe, exquisite fruit flavours.

Within Europe the character of Rieslings is determined by where they are produced. On the Mosel they are so delicate; on the Rhine fuller bodied. In Alsace they are firmer and more phenolic: In Austria they have a mineral backbone similar to the so-called 'hard rock' mineral slate Rieslings of the Clare Valley.

Leo Buring (1876-1961) was the first Australian vintner to make fine Rieslings and his precise methods have been widely followed by fellow Eden Valley producers, such as Yalumba (Contours), Orlando (Steingarten) and the Grosset/Hill Smith partnership that produces Mesh. However, there are two main differences from Buring's heyday. Modern equipment is now used to chill and clarify the must before reductive fermentation which is often initiated with cultured yeasts: and screwcap closures are now preferred to cork to retain freshness and keep the wines in perfect condition.

Clare Valley Rieslings have extraordinary purity and precision. They are marvellous to drink when young and fresh, but after the first year or so, they can go into hibernation, re-emerging as mature wines several years later. After nine or ten years in bottle they are wonderful to drink and their freshness often lasts for 20 years or so.

Elsewhere in Australia, Tasmania's Tamar Ridge produces very fine Riesling in its Kayena vineyard: in Victoria the most notable Riesling I tasted was Crawford River's Condah: in Western Australia, Frankland Estate produces top notch Riesling. By the time you read this I am sure there will be new sources and new producers because the future for Australian Riesling looks very promising. It is an ideal wine for those living in warmer climates close to an abundant source of fresh seafood such as those of South East Asia. Every time I visit

Sydney almost the first thing I do is take the harbour ferry down to Doyles Fish Restaurant, find a waterside table, order fresh fish and Clare or Eden Valley Riesling and watch the world go by. For me it is one of life's greatest pleasures! Clare and Eden Valleys set the pace for Australian Riesling but there are also fine Rieslings made in Tasmania and Western Australia.

GROSSET

Jeffrey Grosset's unswerving dedication to his craft and his relentless pursuit of excellence has helped make Clare Riesling a name to be reckoned with in the world of fine wine.

Grosset also deserves recognition as one of the prime movers along with Yalumba) in the introduction of screwcap closures. When the same Riesling with several years of bottle age closed with a screwcap is compared with the identical wine closed with cork, it is easy to understand why the Clare Valley producers were so determined to champion screwcap closures. Wines bottled with screwcaps are purer, fresher and better. Grosset summed up succinctly: 'We no longer have to pour good wine down the drain because it has been ruined by poor cork'. At its worst, cork taint meant the loss of between 5% and 10% of bottles of fine wine.

Every Grosset wine is polished and pristine. His splendid 2008 Springvale Watervale single vineyard Riesling is a model of composure and length, while his Polish Hill Rieslings are flinty and firm: they can be austere when young, yet they blossom with age and assume a wonderfully persona in maturity.

Grosset also jointly produces a classy Eden Valley Riesling with Robert Hill Smith of Yalumba under The Mesh label. The combination of ideas, skills and knowledge of two great winemakers makes a fascinating, top quality wine. Look out for this special celebration of Riesling.

I tend to think of Jeffrey Gosset as a Riesling specialist, but he also produces outstanding reds. His 2005 Grosset Gaia, a single vineyard blend of Cabernet Sauvignon and Merlot, is beautifully layered with different flavours and great complexity. His rich and elegant Pinot Noir, sourced from grapes in the Adelaide Hills, is a classic. Piccadilly Valley sources the grapes for his accomplished Chardonnay, yet another extremely good and different example of the variety.

When asked what he considered makes his wines so outstanding – Langtons list his Riesling as one of Australia's 17 most Exceptional wines - Grosset gave a one word answer: 'Pangkarra.' Having reduced an ignorant hack to silence he explained that pangkarra is the aboriginal word for terroir- the combination of geology, climate, drainage, angle of slope etc. 'The key to making great, as distinct from good wine, is finding exceptional vineyards and planting them with the right variety for that site. Once we have the right vines in the right sites we can direct our viticultural effort to achieving their optimum performance.' It was a privilege and a pleasure to meet such a fine winemaker at the top of his game and to taste his glorious wines.

JIM BARRY WINES

Peter Barry, the current Managing Director, shares Jeffrey Grosset's enthusiasm for screwcaps. He provided three samples of the same Barry Riesling wine bottled nine years previously. The freshest, most aromatic and most pleasing of the samples had been closed with a screwcap, the two other samples with cork.

Barry wanted to make the point about freshness because he values it so highly. The shale top-soil over old limestone, higher rainfall and cool temperatures of the Clare Valley promote freshness, and he wants to preserve it as well as he can in his top of the range Riesling made from the best parcels of grapes from the Florita vineyard.

Jim Barry, the founder of the business, was a good all round sportsman who loved cricket and racehorses. His interest in cricket is revealed in the names he chose for some of his top Cabernet Sauvignon wines. There is a Cover Drive, a First Eleven and a Silly Mid On, the last mentioned – a Sauvignon Blanc-Semillon blend – possibly made with the girlfriends of the first eleven in mind! Jim

Barry's best Cabernet comes from the 14 hectares in Coonawarra, from the old cricket ground vineyard!

Altogether the winery has 200 hectares in ten locations in the Clare Valley and is now self-sufficient in grapes. The most famous Jim Barry wine is the Armagh Clare Valley Shiraz, a single vineyard wine made on land first planted by Irish settlers who named it after their birthplace. The Shiraz clones, originally sourced in Israel, produce low yields of highly concentrated fruit which impressed Robert Parker as well as Australian connoisseurs. It is rated 'outstanding' in Langton's Classification. The 2004 is a huge wine that Peter Barry considers best left a while in bottle. It is an excellent example of Clare Valley Shiraz.

SKILLOGALEE

Dave and Dan Palmer met us in their vineyard, one of the highest in the Clare Valley. Welsh born David admits to a long slow apprenticeship in the wine business having been a senior management consultant until he bought the winery in 1989. His son Daniel, however, has grown up on the estate and went to college locally to hone his winemaking skills. Together they are making opulent, award winning wines from their versatile vineyards.

Dave explained the winery name. 'Pioneers exploring the Flinders Ranges were beset by illness, injury and war-like aboriginals. Having run out of provisions they survived by making a thin gruel made from grass seeds and water. It was known as skillogalee'.

There is nothing thin and watery about the Skillogalee wines which are further proof of the versatility of the Clare Valley. Skillogalee Riesling and Shiraz have won Decanter silver medals: they also picked up gold at the Clare Valley Wine Show where they were up against some pretty smart competition. The 2004 The Cabernets is also a gold medal winning wine.

Riesling, Shiraz and Cabernet Sauvignon account for most of the 50 hectares planted so it was a pleasant surprise to find that the Palmers also produce a luscious late harvest apricot-flavoured Muscat.

However, since ours was essentially a Riesling mission we focused on them over lunch in the Skillogalee Restaurant run by

Diane Palmer. Diane started out with the straightforward idea of serving meals to winery visitors, but her award winning restaurant attracts year round custom.

We tasted Skillogalee's excellent crisp, dry Rieslings alongside those from Leasingham and Knappstein Lenswood Vineyards, with fresh asparagus, crispy prosciutto, and parmesan with a sublime balsamic and olive oil dressing.

The 2004 Skillogalee The Cabernets was perfectly paired with herb-crusted Burra lamb, served with baby potatoes, green beans and sun dried tomatoes. Here we are in Riesling country drinking outstanding Cabernet. What next? The answer was an intensely aromatic and delicious Gewürztraminer.

The Palmers are an industrious family. The men make the wine, daughter Nicola manages the Cellar Door, while Diane not only runs the restaurant but oversees rental of the top quality self-catering accommodation - two purpose built cottages and a spacious, well-furnished three bed-roomed stone farmhouse.

MITCHELLS

Andrew and Jane Mitchell established their winery in 1975 and have become one of the stalwarts of the region producing long lived Rieslings in their old stone apple shed winery which despite its name has been given a five start rating by James Halliday.

This is one of the wineries I definitely intend to visit on my return to the Clare Valley because their whole range of carefully made wines which includes a glorious Cabernet Sauvignon and an elegant Shiraz, have enormous appeal.

PIKES

Andrew and Neil Pike's ancestors came from Dorset although they confess they know little of the early family history. What Andrew, the viticulturalist, does know is that if he plants his Riesling in an east-west alignment, he can better manage the vine canopy and ensure that his grapes do not get scorched in hot weather.

Pikes best fruit comes from Auburn. In 2002 it was very good; in 2005 it was very, very good and in 2008 it was 'bloody marvellous.' The Pikes Traditional Riesling 2008 is an absolute beauty with pure citrus, apple and mineral characters and an elegant, crisp palate. Pikes 2008 The Mullett is an intriguing Riesling/Viognier/Sauvignon Blanc/Chenin Blanc blend.

Andrew took us to the see the remarkable outcropping of old blue slate that makes the soil on Polish Hill so special. Most of the vines are own-rooted and well suited to the organic practices that help to keep the troublesome light brown apple-moth under control.

Pikes also produce Eastside Shiraz. The 2006 was rich with ripe blackberry and mulberry flavours, another stylish Clare red wine.

WAKEFIELD WINES

Wakefield Wines are based in the Wakefield Valley near Auburn, one of the prettiest valleys you will see in Australia.

But Bill Taylor did not choose the location for its picturesque views. As a wine merchant in Sydney importing the finest Bordeaux reds he developed a liking for them and, like Max Schubert of Penfolds, wanted to try and produce wines of similar quality in Australia. In 1969 he purchased 178 hectares of land with old *terra rossa* soils in the Clare Valley and planted Cabernet Sauvignon in the most sheltered sites and was rewarded with the ripe, small-berried fruit perfect for making fine wine.

His decision was vindicated when the first wine they produced in 1973 won the top prize for Cabernet Sauvignon in the Adelaide Show. Since then the company has continued to produce good quality Cabernets, Riesling and Shiraz under their flagship St Andrews label.

Mitchell Taylor, a founding Director of Australia's First Families of Wine, ensures that quality standards are maintained by placing a great deal of responsibility on his vineyard management team under Ken Noak. Colin Hinze, chief viticulturalist works closely with winemaker Adam Eggins to produce three ranges of wines for worldwide distribution. At home the wines are sold under the Taylor family name but in export markets the Wakefield label is used to avoid confusion with Constellation Wines popular priced range under the Taylor name in the USA, and Taylor's Port, so long established in Europe.

With 500 hectares under vine Taylors /Wakefield is by far the biggest producer in the Clare Valley. Well known for its value-for-money wines the company has made a big effort to introduce its more crafted wines to customers at home and throughout the world.

SOUTH AUSTRALIA RED WINE

McLAREN VALE

McLaren Vale, 25 miles south of Adelaide, is the centre of an idyllic region where the foothills of the Mount Lofty Ranges roll down to the blue waters of the Gulf of St Vincent, providing excellent conditions for growing healthy grapes for wine.

Winters are moderately rainy, warm summers are tempered by ocean breezes and long, sunny autumns help the grapes to ripen gradually. The soil is loamy sand over limestone. An environmental management plan has made McLaren Vale, one of the 'greenest' wine regions in the country, a paradigm.

Famous for its olive groves and almond trees - always a sign of generous warmth - McLaren Vale has abundant fruit orchards where apricot, nectarine, peaches, apples and pears flourish.

John Reynell, an early pioneer, gave a start to a newly arrived twenty year old Devon farmer's son named Thomas Hardy who went on to build one of Australia's leading wine companies, until recently part of Constellation Wines, the world's largest wine-making group. The Vale is still dominated by family firms whether growers or vintners, which probably accounts for the wonderful community spirit so evident to visitors.

The region is well known for its Shiraz which accounts for most of the plantings. However, McLaren Vale is also home to the bush vine Grenache, a variety first grown in Australia to make tonic wine for the anaemic, and then port-style fortified wines for the thirsty. More recently it has come into its own as a table wine and it clearly likes the sandy gravel and ironstone soil and climatic conditions.

McLaren Vale is also pretty good for other red varieties such as the Cabernets, Sangiovese and Tempranillo. When phylloxera was rampant elsewhere, South Australia discouraged the introduction of new varieties into the phylloxera free region, but now that its threat can be contained, Vale winemakers are very keen to experiment with other red and white varieties, particularly proven drought resistant varieties from the warmer parts of Europe.

GEMTREE

The 134 hectare Gemtree estate is owned by the Buttery family, third generation grape growers. Melissa, the daughter of the current owner Mike Buttery, is the viticulturalist and is married to winemaker Mike Brown. Melissa's brother Andrew is general manager and his

wife Helen oversees marketing and sales, making it a true family business.

The Gemtree Wetlands comprise a 10 acre bio-diverse area dedicated to native flora and fauna. Created by Melissa Brown with the help of Greening Australia, the project entailed planting 20,000 native trees and constructing six dams to encourage inhabitation by birds, frogs and other wild life. The plan is to develop an eco-friendly walking trail in support of the South Australian Government's broader educational plan.

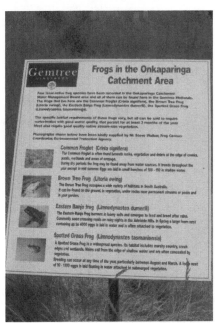

The Gemtree team favours biodynamic farming because it achieves greater phenolic ripeness in black grapes at lower sugar levels, allowing them to be harvested earlier with higher acidity, lower alcohol, greater flavour, and better balance. And also because biodynamic farming maintains more pro-active soils, produces more healthy grapes enabling Mike Brown to make more subtle and distinctive wines.

Mike and Melissa Brown, like Stephen and Prue Henschke, are one of a number of highly successful husband and wife teams in the Australian wine industry. They work together to produce a range of stylishly different wines such as their Citrine Chardonnay and zesty Albarino.

They both embrace experimentation. Mike Brown spent some time in Galicia in northern Spain learning from the masters how to produce their thick skinned, multi-pipped Albarino and noted that they harvest the fruit early to retain natural acidity and bottle it as soon as possible.

Gemtree also produces classy Cabernets such as Tatty Road which, despite its local name, has won many admirers for its juicy fruit flavours lifted by a small amount of Petit Verdot. Mike started his winemaking career with d'Arenberg so it is hardly surprising that he makes some accomplished Shiraz. Tadpole is gentle and juicy, Cadenza full-bodied and fruity, while the outstanding Obsidian is made from the very best fruit on the estate. Gemtree is an impressive family business run with energy, enthusiasm, imagination and a great deal of success.

PAXTONS

Paxtons has nurtured vineyards for more than four decades and is widely recognised for the exceptional quality of its grapes. It owns 100 hectares of its own vineyard and manages 400 hectares for other growers. With a more difficult future forecast for specialist growers, David Paxton began making and marketing a range of seven biodynamic wines from his own vineyards. The decision to produce Paxtons own wines has proved successful, judging from the richly flavoured 2007 Quandong Farm Shiraz, and the top-of- the-range 2005 Jones Block Shiraz.

The estate is totally committed to biodynamic farming, having received its NASAA certification in 2010. General Manager and senior viticulturalist Toby Bekkers led us into the vineyards to see how the biodynamic methods were improving the health and vitality of their grapes. Cover crops are planted between vine rows to establish the microbial life that develops soil nutrients: Beehives placed in the vineyards to improve grape pollination: Special composts prepared from manure provided by the company's own herd of Scottish Highland cattle. Toby Bekkers, Paxton's articulate and accomplished viticulturalist, brought home to me how and why Australian have wines have improved so dramatically over the last thirty years or so. It is a question of knowing what makes a real difference and having the skill and professionalism to carry it through. The Paxtons team is a great credit to the industry.

CHAPEL HILL

The old ironstone chapel from which the winery takes its name also served as a village school. Today, Chapel Hill winery not only produces fine wines and runs a first class restaurant but also has also opened a cookery school which organizes wine appreciation courses. We went there for a Shiraz Master Class.

Having warmed up, so to speak, by tasting a flight of McLaren Vale whites which included Gemtree's zesty 2008 Albarino, Chapel Hills' luscious Verdelho, Coriole's attractive Chenin Blanc, and Gemtree's charming Chardonnay Citrine we tasted and compared 14 McLaren Vale Shiraz wines from the 2002-207 vintages.

The Master Class was superbly orchestrated and briskly conducted by Michael Fragos (winemaker at Chapel Hill) and Chester Osborn (D'Arenbergs) and clearly showed how well top class Shiraz develops with ageing, gaining in spiciness, and becoming more savoury with more positive expression of tertiary flavours. The tasting also revealed how McLaren Vale producers have reined back from the big, oaky, over-extracted Shiraz wines of yesteryear in favour of greater definition, subtlety and individual character.

This was a wonderful opportunity to taste some of the region's very best Shiraz wines in the company of two of its leading winemakers and I followed up my good fortune by tasting other magnificent 2004 and 2005 vintage Shiraz wines including Chapel Hills The Vicar, D'Arenbergs The Dead Arm, Kay Brothers Amery Vineyards Block 6, Clarendon Hills Astralis, Lloyds, Fox Creek, Wirra Wirra, Ingoldby, Tintara and Gemtree's Obsidian.

CORIOLE

Mark Lloyd hosted a gathering of Vale winemakers at Cariole to taste a selection of locally grown 'emerging' varieties accompanied by wonderfully crisp home-baked wood-oven pizzas.

Lloyd has established a fattoria type domain at Coriole where he produces olives, olive oil and wine vinegar as well as a fascinating range of wines including his superb Shiraz and many emerging varieties. He has built up an excellent reputation for the quality of his Sangiovese wines and has successfully introduced other less well known Italian white varieties such as Fiano.

For years South Australian wine authorities discouraged the introduction of new varieties because they feared bringing in the root louse phylloxera which had devastated other vineyards in the 1870's. However, when wine enthusiasts began to show interest in varieties other than the established French favourites, South Australian producers found that they were missing out on new and emerging varieties that Spanish, Italian, Hungarian and Greek immigrants were keen to try, so import procedures were relaxed.

The excellent and diverse growing conditions have allowed many different varieties to flourish: Tempranillo from Spain, Albarino from Galicia, Verdelho from Portugal, Fiano, an ancient white variety from Campania in Italy, Sangiovese from Tuscany, Chenin Blanc from South Africa and Zinfandel from California.

Coriole's 2008 Fiano was both a surprise and a delight. Nicely aromatic with spright, natural acids and a floral character that carried through to the palate. Some pressings are put in the barrel during fermentation to generate added richness of flavour. Gemtree's Moonstone Albarino is also a refreshingly different dry white made with natural yeasts only.

There were several Cadenzia wines on offer - Cadenzia being the name that McLaren Vale producers add to their winery name when labelling their Grenache blends in an imaginative attempt to jointly promote that cultivar. For those not of a musical bent, cadenza is the name given to a brief improvisation by operatic singers to demonstrate virtuosity and creativity before the final cadence of an aria. It is a well chosen name because McLaren Vale producers use their virtuosity and creativity to blend around Grenache depending on the best quality grapes harvested in each vintage.

MITOLO

Mitolo is a relatively new winery opened by Frank and Simone Mitolo in 1999 with Ben Glaetzer as partner and winemaker. Mitolo has Italian roots and the founder is a successful agriculturalist and horticulturalist who wanted to make some very special wines. Frank Mitolo has used his resources wisely: he engaged one of the most dynamic of the younger generation of Australian vintners and found a reliable source of top quality grapes in southern McLaren Vale and in the Barossa.

There are three distinct levels of wine made. Jester, from younger vines, are upfront, fruity wines made to be vivacious and fun.

The GAM range (the name comes from the Mitolo children -Gemma Alexander and Marco) are well defined, spicy and intense thanks to 20% of the grapes being dried in the Amarone style.

The flagship wines are the Mitolo Savitar Shiraz and Mitolo Serpico Cabernet Sauvignon. The 2006 wines were sourced from an elite site of low yielding vines in the Chinese Block. They are finely structured, intense and taut and show all the signs of lasting a very long time. They are bold wines with beautiful balance.

Glaetzer, whose family have been long time Barossa winemakers, has deservedly won praise from the industry's foremost critics for the power and presence of his wines. He is a representative of the younger breed of Australian winemakers who travel widely, love food and taste as many other wines from other producer countries as they can. Glaetzer goes to a lot of trouble and expense to get well seasoned stocks of the right oak for each of the wines he makes, and oversees the coopering of the casks ensuring that they are toasted precisely as requested. This is an impressive winery producing fine, contemporary Australian wines.

GRENACHE

Following the Shiraz Master Class, D'Arenberg hosted a splendid tasting of McLaren Vale Grenache wines. A rich and fruity rose from

Samuels Gorge got proceedings under way reminding us just how suitable Grenache is for making this increasingly popular style.

Having tasted many Grenache, Shiraz and Mourvedre (GSM) blends without getting over excited by them, I was extremely grateful to be able to focus on McLaren Vale Grenache on its own and assess for myself how Australians have developed this splendid variety of Spanish origin which has been so successful in Aragon and Catalonia and across the French border in Roussillon.

Guided by the silk-shirted Chester Osborn we learned that Grenache is site and soil sensitive and grows best in lean, nitrous soils where lower yields produce richly concentrated fruit. The best sites are often on windy ridges where poorer clay/stone soils dominate.

Osborn does not fertilize his Grenache vineyards, nor does he grow cover crops between rows because he doesn't want his vines to become too herbaceous, which detracts from the fruit. He likes to see the canopies in his vineyards on the yellow side of green because it is a sign that they have the mineral edge that give his wine 'extra length.' Most of his Grenache grapes come from old bush vines and are juicy with an exotic, spicy character.

Whilst on the subject of old vine Grenache (and other wines labelled 'old vine') I entreat the appropriate international authorities to agree on an acceptable world wide definition of 'old vine,' – a tag that is so often misused. In South Australia, which (like Chile) managed to avoid phylloxera, there are some genuine 100-150 year old vines. Yet some wines are labelled 'old vine' when metaphorically speaking, the vines are still in short trousers at around ten years of age. My view is that the description 'old vine' should not be permitted on a label unless all the vines are at least 40 or 50 years old.

McLaren Vale old bush vine Grenache is genuinely old. Vine vigour is less marked and as a consequence, there are fewer buds, fewer shoots, smaller canopies, smaller berries, and lower yields. The wines are more concentrated, more distinguished and more elegant because the grapes reach full maturity slowly delivering greater intensity of flavour.

Osborn admits that he has inherited his passion for Grenache from his forbears and it has been the foundation of all D'Arenberg red wines since the company opened its winery doors in 1927. He therefore continues to track growers of healthy, dry-farmed old bush vine grapes and to pay them premium prices for sound grapes which make up the house Custodian Grenache, a marvellously hedonistic wine.

Hedonistic is also the word I would choose to describe Chapel Hill's Bush Vine Grenache made from 80 year old, dry-farmed vines. These fabulous old bush vines still produce generous quantities of dry-farmed grapes as the picture shows.

Steve Pannell (pictured above) founder of SC Pannell, is another Grenache enthusiast. He believes that the cooling sea breezes, that keep the grapes at around 14 Baume for 15 or so days while the tannins ripen fully, are a major factor in the success of his wines. Not that Steve, a longboard surfer who loves the ocean, needs much to persuade him to get down to the beach on a windy day. Son of Dr Pannell of Moss Wood (Western Australia) fame, Steve came east to work at Hardys before extending his experience with winemaking stints in Bordeaux, Burgundy and Barolo. His talent shines through in his wonderfully crafted and hugely impressive wines. His Grenache varietal and Shiraz-Grenache blend are superb wines vinified in small concrete vats and aged in two year old French barrels because the thin skinned Grenache does not take easily to new oak. Another of Australia's most brilliant winemakers.

Roman Bratasiuk at Clarendon Hills also makes very expressive old vine Grenache. Bratasiuk, who arrived from the Ukraine with his parents in 1950, has devoted his whole winemaking life to what he calls varietal expressionism producing 16 different single vineyard wines. Six of which were planted to bush vine Grenache in the 1920s. Romas, his flagship Grenache, comes from un-trellised, ungrafted bush vines on the steepest part of his Blewitt Springs vineyard. He prefers natural yeasts, practices minimal intervention, uses two year old oak barrels, and doesn't fine or filter. No wonder he makes memorable and compelling wines.

Justin McNamee of Samuels Gorge described his 2006 Grenache as being 'like a punnet of fresh strawberries tossed in balsamic vinegar with a little dung.' My look of surprise encouraged him to add: 'It has boiled beetroot and black and tan flavours.' I sipped apprehensively, on the look out for the dung and the beetroot, but McNamee implored me to allow the wine to explode in my mouth. There were indeed wonderful fruit flavours in his wine and a softness that I had not expected from his colourful introduction. 'The softness', he explained 'is due to the old bush vines planted in 'blindingly white' sandy soil.' Grenache bush vines are a fascinating subject and seem to attract colourful characters as growers. As you may have gathered McNamee is driven by texture.

As a result of this tasting I have become a convert to Grenache. This was a Damascus Road job and I am grateful to those McLaren Vale Grenache producers that made my conversion so immensely enjoyable. I shall

definitely be taking a fresh look at GSM blends, even if they have been 'trodden' by such dainty feet as those at D'Arrenbergs, also seen on the front cover photograph by Matt Turner.

LIMESTONE COAST CABERNET SAUVIGNON from McLAREN VALE, LANGHORNE CREEK, PADTHAWAY AND COONAWARRA

McLaren Vale is rightly proud of its Shiraz and its Grenache, but its Cabernets are pretty good as well. Some commentators consider McLaren Vale too warm to make fine, elegant Cabernets, but the Vale has many different microclimates, so it really is a question of finding sites for Cabernet that benefit from cooling afternoon sea breezes.

A tasting of eight McLaren Vale Cabernet Sauvignons and three Cabernet based blends provided an opportunity to assess the overall regional performance of the variety. All eleven wines included in the tasting were imbued with Cabernet's classic characteristics — deep colour, dark-fruit aromas, firm structure and good mid-palate richness. The Vale stand-out feature was the freshness of the fruit, most evident in wonderfully elegant John Davey produced Shingleback Block D, the mature D'Arenberg Coppermine Road and the slightly funky, smoky-nosed but delightful Dead Ringer from Wirra Wirra. Gemtree's 2007 Tatty Road Cabernet blend also appealed because it was lifted by some spicy Petit Verdot, which ripens very well in Australia.

Langhorne Creek on the eastern side of the Fleurieu Peninsula is generally a cooler region than McLaren Vale and also produces delicious Cabernets. The Langhorne Creek name is not as well known as McLaren Vale because historically, most of its wines have been blended into successful brands such as Jacobs Creek and Brown Bothers. Ben Glaetzer admires its qualities so much that he, together with four partners, has established his Heartland Wine Company there. Glaetzer believes that the excellence of the Cabernet Sauvignon is largely due to the benign influence of Lake Doctor, aka the cooling ocean breeze that comes off the southern ocean every afternoon just as the vines are seeking respite from the hot sun. Substantial investment in a high-tech irrigation system has helped improve the quality and consistency of the wines which can increasingly be found bottled under the Langhorne Creek name.

The most remarkable feature of the soil on the Limestone Coast is the layer of decomposed limestone with a high level of oxidized iron known as *terra rossa*. It is most famously concentrated in the vineyards on either side of the main road running ten miles south from Coonawarra to

Penola but there are similar shorter ridges of it as far north as Padthaway which was the first limestone rich region to become an alternative to Coonawarra. Hardy's built their Stonehaven winery there, Browns source a lot of their black fruit from there and Oralndo like the quality of the Cabernet for blending into its brands. As a result the region has become an important red wine producer, yielding twice as many tonnes of grapes as the Barossa. Padthaway also produces surprisingly good Chardonnay with fine natural acidity.

Brian Croser marked out Wrattonbully (14 miles north of Coonawarra) as a special site for Cabernet more than 30 years ago while making wine there for Geoff Weaver. However, it was not until early 2003 that he and his partners (Jean-Michel Cazes and Societe Jacques Bollinger) acquired the eight hectare Koppamurra vineyard (now called Whalebone) and produced its first Cabernet-Shiraz blend. The wine, made from old vines, has the hallmark of all Croser wines- smoothness, suppleness, structure and sophistication with the character of classified growth Bordeaux.

At Mount Benson near the coast, the celebrated Rhone valley grower Michel Chapoutier has planted his own French Syrah rootstock to make a stylish and juicy Australian Shiraz at Domaine Tournon. Intensely red in colour, with black fruit and mulberry aromas, it has depth and complexity and lovely soft, discreet tannins. The wine seems to benefit from being made from grapes grown closer to the sea in that it is refreshingly juicy. It was fascinating to be able to compare Domaine Tournon with Chapoutier's Rhone Syrah of the same vintage. They are wines from the same rootstock yet made a world apart. Domaine Tournon is French in style but less concentrated than the Rhone Syrah and is very Australian in texture.

In the same way that the pebble mounds of the Medoc and the Ridge at Monte Bello provide an ideal combination of soil and climatic conditions for growing great Cabernet Sauvignon, so does the Coonawarran terroir. A million years ago the southern coastal region of Australia was covered by sea cut adrift from what is now Adelaide. When the sea receded, it left a mile wide ridge of red-brown topsoil over decomposed old limestone in free draining soils that vine roots could easily penetrate to access the natural water supply in the ground.

Mild Spring weather encourages early growth: warm Summers relieved by cool winds interspersed with light rainfall, ensure gentle ripening: good harvest conditions more often than not, deliver small, ripe, well coloured grapes with a natural balance of acids, alcohols and tannins. Many growers consider that the optimal sunlight in this isolated region is an important factor in balancing fruit and acids.

John Riddoch, a Scots fruit farmer, realized its potential for grape vines and first planted some in 1893. However, since there was little demand for table wine in the first half of the twentieth century, not much was produced until David and Samuel Wynn bought the Riddoch property in 1951 and soon showed that this extraordinary strip of soil could produce excellent, long lasting wines.

A few years ago in London, Wynn's winemaker Sue Hodder conducted a vertical tasting of the better vintages of their Coonawarra Cabernets from 1990. The tasting revealed how well the wines developed in bottle, becoming rounder, softer and more complex and expressing a very distinctive regional character. It helped that the wines were made from the oldest Cabernet rootstock in Australia, and that they were endowed with the qualities for which the variety is renowned - rich dark berry fruit, firm body, sound structure and lively tannins that soften with time. They were what I call classical wines kind, and Hodder's own comment on them was telling: 'they needed very little 'work' in the cellar,' she said.

Wynn's success attracted many other growers to the region. One new grower was Doug Balnaves, a local sheep farmer with a keen interest in wine, who started by growing grapes for Wynns, but had ambitions to make his own wine. He persuaded Peter Bissell to cross the road from Wynns to make some special wines under the Balnaves name.

The 2004 Balnaves Tally Reserve is one of the most complete expressions of solo Cabernet Sauvignon that I have tasted anywhere in the world. Named after the tally kept by sheep shearers (who are paid for the number of sheep sheared) the wine is produced from the best fruit in the vineyard, fermented in open top stainless steel fermenting vessels, with the drawn off juice being gently pressed to ensure soft and velvety tannins. The result is a smooth, seductive, beautiful Cabernet and a great credit to winemaker Peter Bissell.

Wynns and Balnaves are not alone in producing outstanding Coonawarra Cabernets. Katnook, where John Riddock made one of his early vintages in the woolshed, produces superb estate wines. Their Odyssey Cabernet reserve wine stands out for its richness of flavour. The Hollick family's award winning Ravenswood Cabernet, available in their excellent cellar door restaurant, has been successful. Lighter in style it is an elegant wine made to accompany good food. The Parker Coonawarra Estate is now owned by the Rathbone Group. Their 17 hectare vineyard, at the southern end of the *terra rossa* strip, is home to the pretentiously named but very good, First Growth Cabernet Sauvignon. Brian Lynn at Majella is a former grower who now produces some very good wines including Malleea, a super premium red of distinction. Doug Bowen favours late picking on his eponymous estate and the results show in his smooth, subtle, 'smiling' wines. Kym Tolley's Penley Estate produces admirably rich and complex Cabernets. Formerly a Penfolds winemaker he has a wonderful touch and I enjoyed his wines enormously. Zema Estate found on the Riddoch Highway is another source of superbly crafted beautifully balanced wines.

Most of the brand owners source a lot of their Cabernet Sauvignon from Coonawarra. Max Schubert often used the best of Penfold's Coonawarra grapes in Grange, and other top Cabernets and Cabernet blends. Lindemans have won fistfuls of medals for their Coonawarra Cabernets.

Coonawarra Shiraz should by no means be forgotten, nor the many stylish Cabernet-Shiraz blends. Chardonnay and Riesling is also produced well. However, being a Cabernet fan and having tasted exceptional Coonawarra Cabernets, I find it difficult to think of the region in terms of other varieties. There can be few places in the world more suitable for the cultivar than the Red Cigar, the local name for the appellation on account of its cigar shape.

BAROSSA

The Barossa Valley is Australia's most famous wine making region. Its rich heritage derives from the large scale immigration of British and German settlers in the 1830s and 1840s. In the decade or so after the foundation of the new colony more than 500 Silesian Lutheran families came to start a new life in the religiously tolerant State. George Angas, a wealthy British investor in South Australia, chartered four ships to bring families of energetic, hard working and skilful agricultural workers, to develop his land. They settled around Tanunda where the bakery produces German breads and cakes and the butchery sells German sausages and cold cuts.

The Barossa, however, is not named after Silesians but after a small town in southern Spain, the site of a British victory in the Iberian Peninsular War. Colonel Light, the surveyor-general of South Australia at the time, fought in the Battle of Barrossa and so named the new settlement as a tribute to his former colleagues. Interestingly, Barossa was incorrectly spelt at the naming and has never been corrected.

Today the Barossa Valley is arguably rather more famous than the Barrossa battle site near Cadiz.

The European Revolutions of 1848 brought a second wave of immigration to the region. English speakers settled around Angastown named after its promoter. One of these new immigrants was Samuel Smith, a brewer from Dorset, who established Yalumba, the oldest family-owned wine business in the Barossa.

Gently rolling hills and transverse valleys provide a range of different and fertile soils for both red and white varieties. It is a hot dry climate and is dependent on irrigation, although many of the best vineyards on flatlands in the area around Ebenezer village are dry-farmed.

Shiraz dominates the plantings and thanks to Lehmann and Co there are still many marvellous old vine vineyards. There are also some very fine Cabernet vineyards from which Penfolds source grapes for Grange. Chardonnay and Semillon are prominent on the valley floor and Riesling in the Higher Eden Valley.

SHIRAZ

Shiraz, called Hermitage when it first arrived in Australia in 1832 with the Busby collection, has been at home in the warm dry climate ever since. It is by far the most widely planted variety in Australia (44,000 hectares) and has proved its versatile nature by making elegant, peppery meaty, cool climate wines in Victoria; chocolaty wines in McLaren Vale; intensely flavoured and spicy wines on the Limestone Coast and in Margaret River; rich and leathery wines in the Hunter Valley and dark, muscular ones in the Barossa. Cool climate Shiraz grown in the Adelaide Hills, Eden and Clare Valleys and at Mount Benson shows intense fruit flavours and has a longer palate.

It seems that the cool climate, lighter style is gaining in popularity over the old ferruginous style that one critic has likened to 'a three course meal.' Cool climate wines are more floral on the nose, medium bodied, more exotic and savoury on the palate with good acidity and fine-grained tannins that make them much more food-friendly.

For a long time Shiraz was considered a workhorse variety that produced strong 'gutsy' fortified wines and was often sold as Australian Burgundy. There was so little demand for it that in the 1970s that the South Australian Government initiated a vine pull scheme to replace it with the more fashionable Cab-Savs and Chardonnay.

However, a number of Barossa growers marshalled by Peter Lehmann, did what they could to save the marvellous old, in some cases, pre-phylloxera, vines. They proceeded to show the world what wonderful wines could be made from them. Since then Shiraz has become the most precious jewel in the Australian wine crown, earning extravagant praise from such important critics as Robert Parker and French Rhone Valley growers such as Michel Chapoutier and the late Gerard Jaboulet. Chapoutier was so impressed that he purchased Domaine Tournon at Mount Benson on the Limestone Coast to produce Australian Shiraz from his own French Syrah clones. While Jaboulet mused aloud that Australian Shiraz was so good that the Aussies should keep it for themselves and give the French a chance to sell theirs.

Wine critics praised the 'orange peel and damson aromas, liquorice and white pepper touches, chocolate and mocha sweetness.' Since then Australian Shiraz has become a firm favourite with wine enthusiasts around the world. In Langton's Classification of Australian wines more than one third of the top 120 wines are Shiraz or Shiraz blends. It blends well with Cabernet Sauvignon and several leading vintners consider that well blended Shiraz-Cabernet wines represent the true character of Australian wine.

Despite low yields, viticulturalists have a particular interest in old Shiraz vines because they build up carbohydrates that help the vine perform better in drought conditions, an important consideration as water becomes scarcer. Growers carefully nurse old vines, pruning away sick branches and training the healthy ones on trellis to give them better exposure to the sun, and mulching them with straw to generate microbial life in the surrounding soil.

PETER LEHMANN

Peter Lehmann, often referred to as 'the Bishop of the Barossa,' has long since retired from the company he founded but his spirit lives on through many of the team he recruited who now manage the business, owned by The Hess Group, which also has fine wine interests in France, Argentina and California.

Lehmann was winemaker at Saltram in the early 1970's when there was such little demand for Barossa table wines that his employers told him to cancel all standing orders with red grape suppliers.

Rather than see growers, from whom he had bought grapes for more than twenty years, suffer crippling losses Lehmann formed his own company, borrowed the money to buy the grapes, make the wine himself and sold it. Not surprisingly, the same growers have been loyal to him ever since.

PL, as he is still affectionately known in the trade, used the old vine grapes to produce fine wines that put Australian Shiraz on the wine map of the world. It was the making of the Barossa and quite rightly, the Lehmann name has become one of the strongest premium wine brands in Australia.

The current winemaker Ian Hongell facilitated a wonderfully informative 'Diversity of Shiraz' tasting at which we compared wines from the different sub regions of the Barossa. Appropriately we concluded with a tasting of the very top echelon of Lehmann wines including 2005 The Futures, 2003 Eight Songs and the highly ranked 2002 Stonewell which has superb balance and poise for such a big wine. Watch out for the introduction of more single vineyard Shiraz wines from Ebenezer, Kalimna and Greenford.

CHARLES MELTON

If Graeme Melton is the owner and winemaker, why is he called Charlie and his company called Charles Melton? The answer is that his first boss was Peter Lehmann refused to call him Graeme, insisting on calling him 'Charlie.' Thus Graeme answers to Charlie and to avoid  confusion named his company Charles Melton.

'Charlie' makes 15,000 cases of hand-crafted premium wines a year, mainly from his preferred Rhone varieties. On his first visit to France's Rhone Valley he was immediately attracted to the Chateauneuf du Pape wines and determined to try and produce an Aussie version. He copied French methods, pruning severely to control yields, and picking early to ensure good levels of acidity.

His 20 hectare estate now produces about a third of his annual grape requirement so he contracts for the balance from established growers. He purchases dry-farmed grapes from the Barossa's cooler sites because the lower yields produce more elegant and stylish wines.

In the cellar he processes by whole bunch fermentation in open top fermenters, using indigenous yeasts. He practices *pigeage,* punching down the cap to aerate the must and extract colour and tannin.

It is advisable to be careful when 'Charlie' uses French words like *pigeage.* His best known red wine is a blend named Nine Popes because he thought that Chateauneuf du Pape translated as 'the castle of nine popes' and since he could not use the appellation Chateauneuf he settled for the Nine Popes bit!

However, there is no mistaking the quality of the 2006 Nine Popes, musky on the nose with plump Grenache fruit, trim tannins and a firm backbone. Most of the fruit comes from 130 year old vines and the wine matures *'sur lie'* in the Rhone style.

When it comes to naming his blends, Charlie seems to favour the spiritual theme: Voices of Angels (smooth and harmonious with plush fruit flavours) and Grains of Paradise (smooth, stylish, top-end Barossa) make up a heavenly trio with Nine Popes. His handling of bush vine Grenache is masterful and he produces a lovely juicy, fruity wine he calls Richelieu after the Cardinal. His deep-coloured, rich and spicy Virginia Rosé is made from Grenache and Cabernet Sauvignon.

ST HALLETT

A loud squawk greeted our arrival at the St Hallett winery. Stuey the parrot was on cellar door duty and announced us to his boss Stuart Blackwell who has been making wine at St Hallett for thirty-odd years. When the owner decided to switch from fortified to table wine production in the 1980s he brought in Bob McLean to help with marketing the transition and the management duo concentrated their efforts on building a range of stylish, full-bodied reds from the Barossa, and fine Rieslings from the Eden Valley.

They established the St Hallett brand so successfully that it attracted the attention of the Lion Nathan group, at which point Bob McLean went his own way while Stuart Blackwell stayed on to oversee the company's further development as a sound medium-sized business producing 100,000 cases a year.

Blackwell proudly showed the current range of Eden Valley Rieslings made from 85 year old vines. I liked the basic 2008 Riesling which is lifted by 7g/1 residual sugar. Poachers Reserve, a blend of Riesling, Semillon and Sauvignon Blanc, also has a little residual sugar yet it is crisp and fruity, a joy to taste in the latter part of a busy morning!

Wherever there is a poacher sooner or later a gamekeeper will show up. Gamekeeper is the name given to a smoky-nosed Grenache-Shiraz blend imaginatively spiced up with a touch of Tauriga Nacional.

St Hallett makes three Shiraz wines-Faith, dark and resolute: Blackwell (named after Stuart) bold and assertive: Old Block Shiraz, deep and complex from vines planted in

1913. Old Block Shiraz is one of the most sought after Shiraz wines in Australia.

During our visit Bob McLean called in to see his former colleague and shared a glass of his Menglers Hill Riesling with us. Known locally as the Jolly Green Giant because of his rumbustiuous character, large frame and penchant for dark green suits, Bob is one of those larger-than-life characters that helped make the Barossa famous.

TURKEY FLAT

Peter Schulz's ancestors named the company after the bush turkeys that wander freely across the family vineyards first planted with Shiraz 158 years ago. Peter, the fourth generation of the Schulz family to grow grapes in the Barossa, believes that his role in life is to preserve and enhance the 24 hectares of unique soils and vines for the fifth generation! Meanwhile he makes some very fine wines of his own.

Chair of the Barossa Tourism Board and a member of the Wine Federation Board Schulz naturally champions the Barossa and his varietal wines reflect its generous character. With his wife Christie, an accomplished wine maker, they produce very polished Shiraz/Grenache blend as well as his trade mark Shiraz. However, the wine that left its mark in my memory is the 2006 Mourvedre, one of the most complete and satisfying samples of the variety I have yet tasted. Made from very old vines it is further evidence of how well Rhone varieties have established themselves in South Australia and Victoria.

To round off the tasting Schulz poured a glass of his Pedro Ximinez, a rich and exotic wine made from the grape most associated with Jerez de la Frontera, but quite widely planted in Australia when fortified wines ruled the roost. It was a very pleasant reminder of the Barossa's rich heritage.

YALUMBA

Yalumba is the largest family owned business in the Barossa established in 1849 when Samuel Smith, a master brewer from Dorset, arrived in the Barossa with his family to start a new life.

I have already described Yalumba's activity in the Eden Valley but the company merits close attention for its fine record of achievement in many fields within the industry- pioneering new varieties, developing its own nursery and cooperage, its leadership in green house gas management and campaigning to raise standards of winemaking, packaging and labelling.

Robert Hill Smith (right) the current Chief Executive, inherited the pioneering spirit of his ancestors and has made some bold decisions of his own. In 1992 he sold off Yalumba's fortified wine portfolio to concentrate on developing a range of top quality table and sparkling wines. With the proceeds of the sale he modernized the Angaston winery and extended the company's vineyard holdings in  Coonawarra and Tasmania, also buying the Jansz brand of sparkling wine. Together with Brian Walsh he pioneered the production of Viognier in Australia which his Chief Winemaker Louisa Rose has done so much to advance.

124

The Yalumba Nursery, first established in 1974 to help the company become self sufficient in supply of reliable rootstock and bench grafted vines, has been developed to become one of the largest and most respected in Australia. With new, state-of-the-art facilities it can produce more than a million bench grafts each year. These are mostly sold to high end producers who understand the importance of the latest clonal material in delivering better and healthier fruit. The Nursery also caters for the current interest in emerging varieties such as Tempranillo, Sangiovese, Petit Verdot, Albarino and Fiano.

Tim Jones, the nursery production manager, has several research projects on the go including measuring the flavour performance of different clones in Barossa's various soil and climatic conditions; testing clonal material best able to cope with increasingly saline soil conditions; and conducting tests to find the best means of controlling the troublesome light brown apple moth. At the same time the nursery is also making a determined attempt to bring back bush vine species.

Yalumba is the only Australian winery with its own fully operational on-site cooperage. Because oak plays such an

important part in the ageing of Barossa red wines, the management determined to secure supply of the very best oak barrels. The cooperage imports French and American staves, seasons them thoroughly in the open air to leach away any bitter character in the wood, and coopers them on site, toasting them as required to impart the rich chocolate mocha characters that add texture to big Shiraz wines without masking their fruit flavours.

In 1976 Yalumba took the brave decision to bottle half of its Riesling production with screwcap closures. Unfortunately, consumers at that time assumed that any wine bottled without a traditional cork must somehow be inferior. Nevertheless, Yalumba (and other leading Clare Valley producers such as Grosset) persisted in demonstrating the advantages of screwcap closures over cork and their patient crusading has paid off as modern consumers now prefer screwcaps for such fragrant wines.

Brian Walsh, one of the quieter, more thoughtful and more accomplished of the Barossa winemakers, organised a composite tasting of the Pewsey Vale Rieslings, Viognier, Chardonnays and the Yalumba range of Barossa red wines.

The red wine tasting began with three single vineyard 2003 Shiraz wines. Hahn Farm, Fromm and Swingbridge from the Eden Valley are all rich and full-bodied but the sheer juiciness of the Swingbridge gave it extra vitality.

I was keen to taste the Shiraz-Cabernet blends which Walsh considers best represent the classic Aussie red wine style. First up was an inky black, dark-berry, fruit flavoured wine appropriately named The Scribbler, followed by The Signature, another top quality 2004 vintage blend showing the advantages of bottle ageing. I first heard about the practice of blending Cabernet Sauvignon with Syrah during my student days in Bordeaux. Before the introduction of Appellation Controlee in France, Hermitage was often used to bolster 'thin' Bordeaux wines, which honest merchants considered to be a good rather than a disreputable practice providing the wine was correctly labelled. Incidentally, Chateau Palmer has recently released a Bordeaux wine in its Nineteenth Century series that is a blend of Cabernet Sauvignon, Merlot and Syrah.

Because Syrah was known as Hermitage in Bordeaux Max Schubert decided to call his new Bordeaux styled wine Grange Hermitage, Grange being the name of Dr Penfold's surgery, and Hermitage being Syrah – which in Australia is Shiraz. I will stop the explanation here because Murphy has a Law which states: 'in trying to make something absolutely clear, someone will be confused!'

Why is Hermitage or Syrah or Shiraz so complimentary to Cabernet Sauvignon? The Bordelais suggest that Syrah adds warmth and vigour to the more rigid Cabernet. Brian Walsh believes that Cabernet fleshes out Shiraz giving it greater flavour and complexity. I like the juiciness and sweetness of old vine Shiraz.

Yalumba's flagship Shiraz is Octavius made from selected bunches from some of its oldest vines. The 2005 vintage has a pleasantly plummy nose, enormous depth and intensity, very refined tannins and a velvety smooth finish. It was a gloriously juicy wine and a fitting finale to a well-organized visit, and memorably juicy barbecued steaks.

BAROSSA VALLEY ESTATES

Barossa Valley Estates (BVE) is a co-operative of 80 Barossa growers formed in 1984 in response to the South Australian Government's call to pull their old Shiraz vines. BVE is an equal partnership with Constellation Wines, managed by Stuart Bourne, an experienced winemaker and Shiraz enthusiast with a somewhat colourful turn of phrase. Bourne whisked us through the modern winery to the tasting room where he had prepared a tasting of all the building blocks he uses to blend BVE's iconic E & E Black Pepper Shiraz.

E & E is a benchmark wine because of its consistency. Only parcels of the most succulent fruit are selected for the blend, most it coming from old, dry-farmed vines. The art of blending (or *assemblage* as the French call it) is based on knowing the character of each and every parcel of wine and how they will react with each other. It was a privilege as well as wonderful education to be able to taste vat samples from individual blocks with Stuart Bourne because he explained his thought processes as he went along and explained how he reached his final decisions on which vats to use and in what proportion.

BVE make a range of other fine Shiraz wines. Ebenezer, named after the village that is one of the most reliable sources for old vine Shiraz in the Barossa, is richly smooth and sublime. Bass, named after the most valuable musical instrument in the local brass band that plays in praise of Shiraz at wine festivals, played some high notes with its superb fruit.

Bourne had also prepared samples of the same Shiraz matured in both French and American oak. It was fascinating to see the differences that the two different woods bring to bear on the same wine. That matured in American oak had sweet vanillin, coconut and mocha notes on the nose, plum and cherry flavours on the palate: the wine matured in French oak was more meaty and spicy with a positive black-fruit flavour. This exercise helped me better understand why Australians generally prefer American oak for Shiraz.

ORLANDO-WYNDHAMS

On arrival at Orlando-Wyndhams, the proprietors of Jacobs Creek, we went as millions of other visitors to the winery do, to have a look at 'the creek that flooded the world with wine' as an enthusiastic publicist once described it.

The brand's phenomenal success has

been built on giving consumers excellent value for their money- well-made, utterly reliable wines at affordable prices. There are 13 wines in the Jacobs Creek Classic range, 5 sparkling wines, as well as top-end Reserve and Heritage wines. James Halliday, the leading Australian wine critic, describes the standard of all the wines as being of 'exemplary' quality. Wine Show judges tend to agree: since it was first launched in 1975 Jacobs Creek wines have won hundreds of Show medals in blind tastings at home and abroad. They still do.

The Jacobs Creek brand, marketed with flair, was proclaimed as 'Australia's Top Drop' and has since become a 'top drop' in the UK, USA and some sixty other export markets.

At the time of our visit senior winemaker Rebekah Richardson was planning the blend of the flagship Jacobs Creek Johann Shiraz Cabinet, one of five super premium wines in the range, and invited us to take part in a similar blending exercise. We were divided into three groups, each equipped with calibrated test tubes and six samples (one Cabernet Sauvignon and five Shiraz wines) from different sources. Our task was to make up three blends from the samples, noting the proportions of each wine used.

Given that our group included two Masters of Wine, two others with winemaking experience, three senior wine educators and a couple of experienced hacks, we relished the challenge. We began by assessing the characteristics of each of the individual wines before trying out possible combinations.

'Let's start with a generous portion of Cabernet Sauvignon to give the blend sound structure,' suggested one of our team. 'Yes, but not too much,' argued another while the third team member suggested that sample 3 would be better than sample 5. To cut a long story short, when we had completed the task, Rebekah told us that we had turned out to be just like any other group of blenders-argumentative, opinionated and pushy!

Phil Laffer Orlando's long serving Director of Wine, is one of the most respected blenders in the industry. He believes that brands are only as good as the grapes that go into them. That is why he encourages the 20 strong team of winemakers to focus on finding the very best parcels of grapes from wherever they find them.

Our reward for taking part in the blending exercise was a glass of 2008 Jacobs Creek Reserve Riesling followed by the single vineyard 2003 Jacobs Creek Steingarten, both sourced from the Eden Valley, both served with fresh oysters and both enjoyed enormously. More wonderful sea food including Morton Bay Bugs,

Scallops and King Prawns was served with 1997 Steingarten - mature Australian Riesling at its very best. Steingarten Riesling proudly takes its place in the line up of Heritage wines alongside Reeves Point Chardonnay, St Hugo Cabernet Sauvignon, Jacobs Creek Shiraz and Johann Shiraz-Cabernet.

PENFOLDS

Visiting Magill Estate, seeing the original Grange homestead where Dr Christopher Penfold lived and practiced as a physician, and what remains of the Magill vineyards, viewing the old winery (still in use) and tasting the iconic Penfolds Grange was a memorable experience – and a superb history lesson!

Over the 166 years of its history Penfolds has acquired some of the very finest vineyards

in the Barossa, McLaren Vale, Clare and Eden Valleys, Coonawarra and the Limestone Coast the absence of the ebullient Head Winemaker Peter Gago, on ambassadorial duty in the USA, we were conducted around the estate by colleagues Jamie Sach and Tom Riley, who gave us a comprehensive tasting of the Penfold range of wines.

We started with an aromatic and zesty Bin 51 Eden Valley Riesling and two Chardonnays from the Adelaide Hills. The Reserve Chardonnay Bin 06 is whole bunch pressed and filled into wood where it undergoes malolactic fermentation. Yattarna, the top-of-the-range Chardonnay that is often referred to as the White Grange, is a wonderfully accomplished wine. The 2004 is multi-layered, mature and magnificent. Class in a glass! The 2006 Cellar Reserve Pinot Noir, another wine sourced from the Adelaide Hills, is made from

hand picked grapes, cold soaked, fermented with selected yeasts, and aged in wood of different ages (of which only 20% was new) before being bottled unfined and unfiltered. This benchmark Australian Pinot Noir underlines the potential of the Adelaide Hills for top quality wines.

The Bin 389 Cabernet-Shiraz has been dubbed 'the poor man's Grange,' because it is matured in barrels used the previous year for Grange. Sourced from several South Australian regions, and harmonized into a beautifully balanced wine with bold fruit flavours and plush tannins it shows the same qualities as a terroir wine. It is of course reasonable to argue that South Australia *is* a terroir. The Comte de Segur once owned 1000 hectares of St Estephe: but only the best grapes went into Calon Segur.

St Henri Shiraz is sometimes called 'the alternative Grange' because it includes wonderful fruit sourced from cooler sites in the Barossa, McLaren Vale and Coonawarra. Senior winemaker John Davoren has succeeded brilliantly in creating a perfumed, elegant wine with well defined fruit flavours as an alternative to the more powerful Grange.

RWT Shiraz, short for Red Winemakers Trial, is mostly sourced from the best northern Barossa vineyards. Its fine aromatics, rich ripe fruit, superb balance and harmony make up for its unfortunate name!

Having started my training in Bordeaux and Burgundy and got used to such romantic names as Leoville Las Cases, Montrose, Chambolle Musigny Les Amoureuses and Corton Charlemagne, I find it quite difficult to generate the same enthusiasm for a wine labelled RWT or a bin number! However I acknowledge that such arcane names are probably the Australian response to the plethora of unpronounceable and often unmemorable village French vineyard names, and that numbers and initials have the same kind of resonance to Australians as such place names do to the French.

Whatever the name or number on the label, Cabernet Sauvignon Bin 707, Kalimna Bin 28 and Coonawarra Bin 128 are magnificent wines and, like most of Penfold's top wines, only produced when there is sufficient top quality fruit available.

It is difficult not to be a little bit overawed when tasting such iconic wines as Grange.

Before picking up my glass of the 2003 vintage I made an effort to clear my mind and concentrate on the wine in front of me. I liked the deep crimson colour. The nose indicated really good fruit and vanillin from the American oak. The palate was sweet and fleshy with dark fruit flavours. The tannins were quite dry. In the discussion afterwards I learnt that 2003 had been a hot but difficult summer which meant multi-district selection of  grapes. The final blend for the 2003 was 96% Shiraz, mostly from Barossa, McLaren Vale and Coonawarra.

Grange has always been about selecting the best grapes available in the vintage, from whichever region/district they may come and from whichever variety performs best in a particular vintage. The aim is always to produce a truly fine wine that will develop the bottle over twenty years or more.

The 1994 Grange served with dinner was quite different from the 2003 as one would expect from a wine with 12 years bottle ageing. The crimson was more muted but the wine showed attractive black fruit aromas with ripe blackberry flavours, fine tannins and a long powerful finish. Made with 89% Shiraz and 11% Cabernet Sauvignon, it is quite beautifully balanced and complete. Hardly surprising when I learned that the grapes came from Penfolds best sites in Barossa, McLaren Vale and Coonawarra. All the Penfolds wines are a credit to the winemaking team under Peter Gago and Grange has clearly justified all the time and work devoted to its introduction and development. It is time to pay homage to Max Schubert, its creator.

MAX SCHUBERT (1915-1994)

Max Schubert, arguably the most important and influential figure in the modern Australian wine industry, was a modest man from a humble background. Yet he led Australia out of the era of 'fourpenny dark' fortified wines into a golden age of fine table wine. He proved to his fellow Australians and wine enthusiasts everywhere, that Australia had the climate and soils to produce world class wines.

Schubert's life is a story of hard work. He began his career with Penfolds as a 16 year old junior laboratory assistant in 1931 developing an interest in the smells and tastes of wine, and studying chemistry at night school. At the age of 21 was made a junior winemaker at Magill, in 1940 he became an assistant winemaker and in 1949 was appointed Chief Winemaker.

Since Penfolds business in the 1950s was based on fortified wine the company sent its Chief Winemaker to study the Spanish and Portuguese winemaking methods used in Jerez and Oporto. Having completed his studies he visited Bordeaux on his way back to Australia, and had the good fortune to be shown around by Christian Cruse, a leading merchant and one of the great gentlemen of the wine trade. Cruse introduced Schubert to the great classed growths and he was deeply impressed with the rich, concentrated and mature wines he tasted. On the way home he determined to try and emulate them, by making Australian wines that would continue to develop in the bottle over 20 years or more.

Back in Australia Schubert began his self appointed task by making a complete survey of all Penfolds vineyards, learning the ripening patterns of each one, and registering the flavours that its vines produced. He was constantly on the look out for blocks of vines and vineyards on which he could depend for top quality grapes. His first efforts underwhelmed his colleagues and after a few years they withdrew their support for the project. With the encouragement of one particular member of the Penfold family he carried on secretly, overcoming periods of doubt, disappointment and despondency to achieve his dream of producing a fine, complex wine that would develop in the bottle.

His experience in Bordeaux had taught him that to make great wine consistently it was necessary to have a reliable source of exceptional grapes. His original intention was to base his blend on Cabernet Sauvignon but since Penfolds had little of it planted he decided on Shiraz which was readily available from Penfolds best vineyards in the Barossa, McLaren Vale, Coonawara and the Clare Valley.

Schubert admired the acid-tannin structure of Shiraz, finding its structural qualities similar to Cabernet Sauvignon, which he also planned to use as and when quality grapes became available. However, from the outset of the Grange project Schubert determined that he would only use phenolically ripe grapes in which there was a natural balance of sugars, acids and tannins, irrespective of their origin. Over the years he came to rely on certain blocks of old vines in the Barossa.

Grange has often been held up as a brand rather than a terroir wine but when the Barossa grapes are at their best, there is little to beat them. Other regions grapes may add a nuance or two but most of the grapes came from tried and tested vineyards that Schubert knew so well.

He made every batch of wine carefully on the grounds that 'wines made with faults stay faulty.' He used many of the winemaking techniques he had learned in Bordeaux and also applied the lessons he had learnt about maturation. He started by using French oak but switched to American because he liked the note of sweetness on the palate. His greatest skill was harmonising flavours that would continue to develop over the years.

It took several years for his colleagues to understand just how successful their Chief Winemaker had been. Within fifty years of his first experimental Grange it was being traded on the Bordeaux market alongside the great classified growth wines he had tasted in 1951.

Max Schubert was awarded the Order of Australia, made Decanter Winemaker of the Year, and was the first winner of the prestigious Maurice O'Shea award for his remarkable work. He gave fellow Australians the confidence to express their own ideas in their winemaking and showed the importance of hard work and self belief if dreams are to be realised.

THE FUTURE OF THE BAROSSA

There is something very special about the Barossa. Its landscape, its microclimates, its wonderful old vines, its legendary viticulturalists and winemakers who have developed the art of blending grapes from different parts of the region to make their super premium blends of Shiraz. It is one of the world's very great wine regions, and visiting it generated in me an enormous admiration and respect for the pioneer settlers who tamed it, located the best viticultural sites, planted and nurtured them; and then the vinyardists who have constantly fought battles against heat, disease and pests and have maintained their vineyards so well that they are still producing sound and healthy fruit. Despite the current difficulties with water supply, the future of the Barossa is in good hands because of the depth of experience, appreciation and affection that growers, winemakers and blenders have for their land and because of the wealth of emerging winemaking talent.

Ben Glaetzer, son of Colin and Judith (reputable winemaker and highly qualified oenologist respectively) is typical of the gifted

148

younger generation of winemakers who have shown that they are capable of taking Barossa wines to new heights. Drawing on exceptional fruit from the famous Ebenezer vineyard in the northern Barossa, Glaetzer produces stunning modern wines such as Amon-Ra Shiraz and Anaperenna a Shiraz -Cabernet blend, which have been lavishly praised by the world's leading wine critics..

Ben Glaetzer took over the family winery in 2002 with the ambition of making what he called 'more global' wines. When asked to explain he said that he hoped to make more contemporary wines, more international in style and better to enjoy with fine cuisine.

Glaetzer is very selective in his use of oak: he likes to discuss his plans for each wine with his chosen cooper to ensure that together the best wood is selcted for each particular wine, and then coopered and toasted according to the character of the wine and the time it will stay in barrel. He intends to make wines that 'stay alive.'

But the future of the Barossa is not only in the hands of the young but in what I call the 'young-old' vintners such as John Duval. For 29 years he served Penfolds, the last 16 as Chief Winemaker in charge of Grange. He now runs his own family business and still loves working with old vine Shiraz. Over the last six years his Entity and Eligo Reserve Shiraz (only made in vintages that produce exceptional fruit) have been given rave reviews.

Members of the Circle of Wine Writers spent a marvellous evening with the Artisans of the Barossa, a lively group of 12 independent winemakers (representing 12 different sub-regions of the Barossa) formed in 2006 to collectively promote their hand crafted wines. They are united in their commitment to further the reputation of the Barossa and its greatest treasures - old vine Shiraz and Grenache.

Many of the Artisans are gifted young winemakers such as Dan Standish, Kym

Teusner and Andrew Wardlaw (left to right in the picture below) who hold down day jobs with established wineries: others are successful businessmen indulging their heartfelt passion for wine.

The structure of the Australian wine trade is quite different from that of most of Europe where owners are often both grower and winemaker, and much more conscious of 'place' than the variety of grape grown. In Australia there are a number of growers who have no ambition whatsoever to become winemakers. They consider themselves to be viticulturalists and concentrate all their energy on growing the best possible grapes – in most cases working closely with the winemakers to whom they normally sell their grapes. There

151

are also oenologists who love making wine but do not   yet aspire to growing grapes or, perhaps nearer   the truth, do not have the capital to buy land and plant it out to the ideal standard.

Young winemakers therefore enjoy the challenge of turning the best grapes that they can buy into a wine that expresses their own ideas of variety and vintage; perhaps adding something of their own personality.

Over an informal supper at Peter Clarke's Vintners Restaurant in Angaston we tasted many of the Artisan's wines.   Conversation flowed like the wine as individual artisans explained his or her own particular approach to winemaking. For example Peter Clarke's Tin Shed Company places emphasis on clear varietal definition and elegance, ensuring his wines suitability for his and other restaurant menus.

Greg Hobbs, formerly an anti-terror policeman in Adelaide, is keen to indulge his passion for making old vine Shiraz: Jason Shwarz, the son of a grower, specialises in old vine Grenache and Shiraz : Troy Kalleske, one of the sixth generation of Silesian settler-farmers, finds winemaking more stimulating than farming: Simon Cowan has committed himself to making world class Rieslings in the Higher Eden Valley: Gill and Ben Radford also make Riesling in the Higher Eden. Their vines are 75 years old. Peter Schell of Spinifex and Dan Standish of Massena have both set their sights on becoming producers of top quality Barossa wines: Kym Teusner makes the wines for Rolf Binder as well as for his own boutique winery. John Edward's Mt Billy was born (in 1999) from one tonne of hand picked 80 year old Grenache: Paul Clancy and Peter Fuller have vowed not to chase fashion, simply to focus on producing authentic Barossa wines. The wines we tasted were sometimes brilliant, sometimes funky, but always interesting, distinctive and different. They certainly add an extra dimension to the overall Barossa offering. If you see their wines around don't hesitate to try them for yourself.

This notebook is not a travel guide but if you visit Australia's wine regions I implore you not to miss the Barossa. It is not only a great vineyard full of history, wonderful characters and some of the very finest wines, better still it is a marvellous base from which to explore all the best South Australian wine regions.

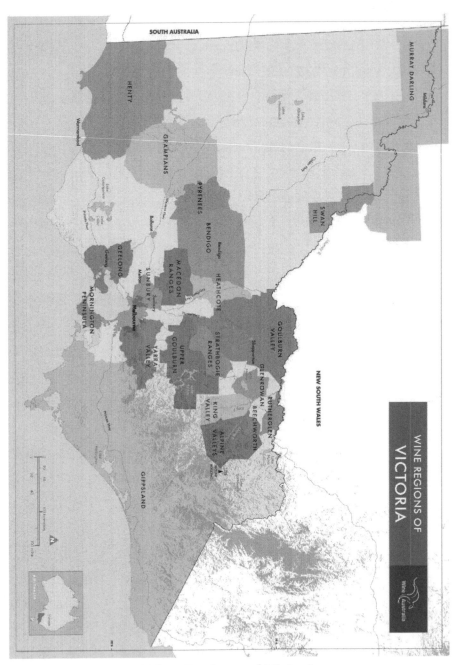

Wine Regions of Victoria

VICTORIA

Victoria, the smallest and coolest of the mainland Australian wine producing regions, is nevertheless only second to South Australia in terms of production. Its diverse soils and microclimates offer a wide range of wines from basic Riverland reds to sophisticated, perfumed Pinot Noirs and silky-smooth Shiraz wines: from full-bodied fruity entry level whites to cultured Chardonnays: from delicious late-harvest 'stickies,' to fortified dessert wines from the dark skinned Muscat; more recently there has been planting of European varieties as Nebbiolo, Sangiovese, Tempranillo, Touriga Nacional, Albarino, Verdelho, even Tannat and Malbec.

The development of the first Victorian vineyards owed a great deal to the discovery of gold at McIvor Creek in 1852, when vines were planted to help slake the thirst of some 40,000 prospectors who came seeking their fortune.

About the same time a group of Swiss vignerons established vineyards at Yering. One of the more ambitious of the group, Hubert de Castellan, believing that Victoria could supply the entire needs of the mother country, set out his plans in *John Bull's Vineyard*. Another, Baron de Pury, planted the first Yarra vineyard at Yeringberg in 1862. However, the gold deposits were soon worked out and when the speculators moved on, most vineyards were abandoned with the notable exception of

Tahbilk, established in 1860 and still thriving as one of the oldest wineries in Australia.

Between 1875-1883 phylloxera devastated those vineyards that remained and in the aftermath, the combination of a poor economy, a domestic temperance movement, two World Wars and a further period of economic instability, meant that few were replanted. Victorian viticultural activity did not revive until the 1960's and then very modestly with only 24 vineyards in the State.

 There were not many more when I first motored up the Yarra Valley in 1983, and one had to look hard to find them. But I did find Dr Bailey Carrodus, a botanist, turned winemaker, who had carried out painstaking research before replanting Yarra Yering vineyard in 1968. He may have looked slightly eccentric with his floppy hat, trimmed grey beard and colourful complexion, but he understood what was necessary to get good fruit and was

absolutely convinced that he could make top quality Australian wines from French varieties. When he succeeded, other small growers poured into the hills northeast of Melbourne, to develop the sub-region.

Things have changed dramatically since then. There are now more than 100 wineries in the Yarra Valley and some 850 in Victoria spread across its 21 district wine regions or Geographical Indicators (GIs) as they are known locally. The real impetus came after 1985 when James Halliday established Coldstream Hills to produce what was described at the time as the 'best white burgundy outside the Cote d'Or', and Champagne Moet & Chandon decided to produce top quality sparkling wine under the Green Point label. Growers sat up and took notice and moved into the valley and beyond.

Unfortunately I do not have the space to fully describe all 21 regions so I have focused on the leading fine wines and winemakers that have proved themselves in recent years.

The Yarra Valley, 25 miles north east of Melbourne, is a useful starting point. Once a lush cattle and sheep rearing valley, it has turned out to be a classic cool climate region with a long gentle growing season. Chardonnay and Pinot Noir quickly made themselves at home in grey-brown loamy soils enriched by decades of sheep manure. In the early 1980s the Burgundian Paul Bouchard was extremely complimentary about its Chardonnays believing that 'they will only get better and better.' He was also charmed by what he called the 'haunting delicacy' of the Pinot Noirs that he tasted.

When I at last followed up his advice to visit I was equally impressed with the smooth, creamy Chardonnays and soft, supple Pinot Noirs. But Dr Carrodus persuaded me that there was a lot more to the Yarra than Chardonnay and Pinot Noir. He believed that he could make Cabernet Sauvignons with the same depth and complexity as the best French appellations and proved his point with fine silky-smooth wines and some excellent Shiraz as well. However, when he found that his customers would pay more for his Pinot Noir, he concentrated his attention on the Burgundian grape.

Dr John Middleton also made a statement with the quality of his wines at Mount Mary. Inspired by the history of the Swiss vintners in the Yarra and having visited major European vineyards, Middleton and his wife Marli planted Chardonnay, Pinot Noir and Cabernet Sauvignon at Lilydale just south of Yering. His Cabernets are intense but always elegant and he seems to have a golden touch with his Pinot Noir. His absolute dedication and that of his son David, has paid dividends. Mount Mary Quintet, is blended from five different Bordeaux varieties, and has become one of the most coveted of all Australian wines, despite the panning it received from Robert Parker. The 2006 Quintet and 2006 Pinot Noir are superb wines but difficult to buy in the market. Mount Mary is a small winery and all its wines are allocated to a long list of dedicated customers. This is also the case with several other small wineries making very fine wines - Giaconda and Bindi immediately spring to mind- so if you are ever offered the chance to taste or buy them do not hesitate.

Coldstream Hills, founded by the wine writer James Halliday (formerly a senior corporate lawyer who started his winemaking experience at Brokenwood in the Hunter valley) is now owned by the Fosters Group Wine Division recently re-named Treasury Wine

160

Estates. Halliday carefully planned the layout of his original vineyard on sloping north-facing land planted with the latest available Dijon clones of Chardonnay and Pinot Noir. In the 1990s I bought Coldstream Chardonnay and Pinot Noir (along with Wynns Cabernet Sauvignon, Michelton Shiraz and Petaluma and Knappstein Rieslings) to introduce my children to Australian wine.

De Bortoli is another prominent family owned Yarra Valley producer. Originally from a small mountain village in northern Italy the De Bortolis have developed their business by making sound wines and dynamic management. The company is now headed by Leanne de Bortoli and her husband Steve Webber, formerly wine maker at Lindemans. Webber knows a thing or two about producing top quality Chardonnay and Pinot Noir and has advanced the company's reputation for producing fine wines such as its outstanding late harvest Semillon Noble One, widely appreciated around the world. Webber also recognizes winemaking talent when he sees it. His white winemaker Sarah Fagan has just been named Young Australian Winemaker of the Year.

Yering Station, owned by the Rathbone Family, is set in a stunning location with its own restaurant and views across the manicured estate now extended by 40 hectares to accommodate the joint venture with Champagne Devaux to produce Yarrabank Sparkling Wine as well as outstanding single vineyard wines chardonnay from Willow Lake and Pinot Noir from Inverness Ridge.

Yarra Yerring, founded by the late Bailey Carrodus, has passed to a new owner who has retained Paul Bridgeman (so carefully selected by Carrodus) as winemaker. Bridgeman continues to produce wines of the highest quality and is one of a number of small boutique wineries whose fine wines are eagerly snapped up by Melbourne's best restaurants and wine merchants.

Phil Sexton took the name for his Giant Steps winery from a song in John Coltrane's first solo album: Sexton personally took giant steps to cross the continent from Margaret River, having sold his Devils Lair winery to Southcorp. He now produces precise terroir driven wines in the centre of Healesville where his cellar door operation boasts a bistro, a wood-fired pizzeria and an artisan bakery. The passionate single vineyard producer becomes entrepreneurial with his share in Innocent Bystander which offers lively, fresh, imaginative wines for newer wine enthusiasts on their way up to single vineyard wines.

McWilliams, one of the larger Australian wine family businesses with vineyards across South Australia, makes subtle and refined Chardonnay and Pinot Noir at their Lilydale vineyards. The cool climate Yarra has proved to be ideal for the Burgundian varieties which have really benefitted from the pioneering work of Carrodus, Halliday and Moet & Chandon.

Heading north from the Yarra, Goulburn is the next great wine growing valley includes the Nagambie Lakes sub-region where the great white and red Rhone varieties thrive. Viognier, Marsanne and Roussanne whites: Shiraz, Grenache and Mouvedre reds. Goulburn also produces long-lasting Cabernets.

The oldest and most famous estate in this region of creeks, lakes and billabongs is named Tahbilk, an aboriginal word meaning 'place of many waterholes.' In 2010 Tahbilk celebrated its 150th birthday. For the last 85 years the family business has been under the shrewd guidance of the Purbrick family, whose pride and joy is a half hectare of ungrafted, 140 year old pre-phylloxera Shiraz vines which produce a few hundred bottles of highly prized 1860 vine Shiraz most years.

Alister Purbrick also produces the outstanding Eric Stevens Shiraz- the 2005 was immense. The winery also owns the world's oldest plantings of Marsanne dating back to 1927, and releases a wine each vintage. I recently tasted the 2001, an absolute treat for aficionados of the variety. The grapes were picked early to retain their natural acids and the freshness of the fruit still shines through. As far as I know, only three other countries in the world produce Marsanne: France, Switzerland and USA. Tahbilk is worth a visit not least for its wine museum as well as its historic vineyards.

I have a soft spot for Mitchelton Wines because the company was my first direct contact with Australian wine. Managed at that time by Colin Preece, another Australian wine legend, the company was named after the explorer who pioneered the overland route between Sydney and Melbourne. The property, bounded on three sides by the Goulburn River, is now owned by the Lion Nathan group. From the outset Michelton's soils and climate favoured Rhone varieties which predominate but their full bodied Cabernets are also brimful of fruit and have admirable staying power. The rich savoury flavours of the beautifully balanced flagship Shiraz linger in my mind.

Heathcote, west of Goulburn, is another sheep-grazing area that has become noted for its rich, velvety, complex, world class Shiraz.

Robert Parker awarded 99 points to the 1997 Duck Muck Shiraz made by Wild Duck Creek Estate, and in so doing brought Australian Shiraz to the attention of US wine drinkers. Duck Muck is only produced in minute quantities in great vintages but it did help bring recognition to other regional growers such as Ron and Elva Laughton and daughters at Jasper Hill. Their top Shiraz is Georgia's Paddock. Sister Emily has her own Paddock which produces a very fine Cabernet Franc, of the more notable I have come across in Australia.

Michel Chapoutier, the famous Rhone valley grower, produces Shiraz at Mount

Benson in South Australia but has invested his time and money in other Shiraz projects. He is associated with the Laughtons and has backed his enthusiasm for Australian Shiraz by making further investment in the region.

Nearby Bendigo (originally part of Heathcote) has also come into the spotlight with the wonderful wines made by Lindsay Ross at Blairgowie Estate, a sumptuous Shiraz and a smooth Cabernet Sauvignon.

South of Heathcote, the Macedon Range producers have earned an excellent reputation for their ultra premium sparkling wines. The coolness of the Ranges generates the acidity which makes their Chardonnays and Rieslings so elegant. Shiraz and Pinot Noir also perform brilliantly in what is probably Australia's coolest region. Bindi's exquisite cherry-flavoured, ultra-concentrated Pinot Noir and its rich, subtle, citrusy Quartz Chardonnay reveal what heights can be reached in Macedon.

Another of Australia's older family wine companies is based in King Valley. Brown Brothers, noted for its exemplary Chardonnay sold at sensible prices, in fact produces a complete range of wines. Their Patricia label has been built by winning customer loyalty and trust.

Brown Brothers, another of Australia's great family wine companies, is based in King Valley and is noted for its exemplary Chardonnay sold at sensible prices along with a complete range of wines the best of which are bottled under their Patricia label.

In 2010 Brown Brothers purchased Tasmania's Tamar Ridge Estate that was built up and run by Dr Andrew Pirie. Commenting on the purchase, CEO Ross Brown (above) recorded his delight at acquiring such fine cool climate vineyards which are a perfect fit with Browns own 700 hectares of warmer sites in upper Victoria. He was particularly pleased to have such an excellent source of top quality Chardonnay grapes for both sparkling and still varietal wines. Brown is equally pleased to have secured such good Pinot Noir plantations, a variety for which he anticipates a promising future.

The road through King Valley continues to Beechworth in the gold digging foothills of the Victorian Alps, once crowded with prospectors. Vines were planted in the 1850s to help slake the thirst of the miners, but they were soon neglected once the seams of the precious mineral were exhausted, and little notice was taken of the region until Rick Kinzbrunner arrived in 1982, took a liking to the fertile, alluvial soils and bought a 6 hectare plot at Giaconda .

Giaconda is one of the many Australian wineries that I look forward to visiting because when I first tasted its citrus flavoured, mineral rich wine Chardonnay I thought I was in heaven.

Rick Kinzbrunner first caught the wine bug in the early 1970's and spent a decade travelling the wine world, studying at University of California Davis, working for Stags Leap in the Napa Valley, Christian Moueix in Pomerol, and Brown Brothers in Victoria before striking out on his own.

His first Giaconda Chardonnay released in 1986, dazzled Show judging panels. Having been trained in Burgundy and spoiled with fine Meursaults, Cortons and Montrachets, I found Giaconda wines to be something else. Distinctive, stylish and gloriously Australian.

Kinzbrunner also makes a marvellous Chardonnay labelled Nantua les Deux which is lifted by a small amount (7% in the 2007) of the exotic Roussane. His ten hectares produce an average of 2,500 cases of wonderfully powerful and complex Chardonnay, Pinot Noir and Cabernets. The downside is that they are difficult to find in the open market, although I have learnt that Berry Brothers and Rudd in London have an allocation.

I have also yet to visit Rutherglen on the border with New South Wales, but having developed a keen interest in Tokaj, I made a point of tasting the luscious, silky dessert wines made from Muscat blended with what used to be called Tokay but which is in fact the Muscadelle of Sauternes. I have to say that the real attraction for me was the unique fortified dessert wines which are one of Australia's most surprising gifts to the wine world. Campbell's Merchant Prince Rare Muscat is exotic and they proudly offer back vintages of these and other similar 'stickies' to Cellar Club members and Cellar Door visitors.

The Grampians, close to border with South Australia, is where the Seppelt family made its name for methode champenoise sparkling wine – and first introduced sparkling Shiraz. The Seppelts, Prussian merchants who settled in the Barossa in 1849 to grow tobacco, soon became more interested in wine and rapidly expanded their business in South Australia before moving across the State border into Victoria. They took over the Great Western Winery building up the sparkling wine business with sound wines matured in its famous underground cellars known as 'The Drives.'

Nearby, at Mount Langi Ghiran (owned by the Rathbone family) Dan Buckle makes fine and elegant Shiraz wines from vineyards nestling under the mountains at the southern end of the Great Dividing Range. The ripening season extends into the autumn encouraging the gentle and gradual development of fruit flavours.

South of Melbourne, Mornington Peninsula encloses Port Philip Bay, famous for its beaches, water sport and tourist attractions. More recently the region has also become noted for the excellence of its Chardonnays and Pinot Noirs. Despite the beaches and water sports it is cooler than the Yarra Valley and as a consequence, its wines are more particular, more precise.

There are now more than 60 wineries on the Peninsula producing well-structured, lean and handsome Chardonnay and Pinot Noir wines from clones that have been selected to accentuate fruit flavours, and encourage complexity and longevity.

Brian Stonier was one of the first on the scene in 1978 and Stoniers (Lion Nathan Group) maintains a very high reputation for distinctive Chardonnay and Pinot Noir. Lindsay McCall at Paringa Estates is recognized for his powerfully scented, sumptuous, silken Pinot Noirs while Merrick Creek, owned by the Parker family (out and out Pinot specialists) has many loyal followers. The Parkers retained Gary Farr as consultant. Renowned for the Pinot he made at Bannockburn, Farr is one of the very top Australian Pinot Noir producers. Trained in Burgundy he recommends careful selection of Dijon clones and the adoption of such Burgundian practices as close-planting Kate McIntyre MW at Moorooduc is also. The Merrick Creek wines are now made by his son Nick. Gary has started his own company appropriately named By Farr.

I warmed to the pleasantly perfumed and earthy McCutcheon single vineyard 2008 Pinot Noir made by Martin Spedding and his crew at Ten Minutes by Tractor, a boutique winery that incorporates the vineyards of three different owners that happen to be ten minutes by tractor from each other. Moorooduc, started by

Richard and Jill McIntyre in 1981 has a growing reputation (and a new Master of Wine, daughter Kate earning that distinction in 2010) as has Mac Forbes, who started at Mount Mary. At Kooyong, planted to Chardonnay and Pinot Noir, Sandro Mosele also produces luscious single vineyard wines. Mosele is of Italian origin and is committed to lower alcohol wines more compatible with fine cuisine since much of Kooyong trade is with high end restaurants which also list fine Burgundies. All these producers are taking Australian Pinot Noirs to new heights, showing that the top Australian wines can stand comparison with some of the longer established Pinot Noir producers.

Some great Pinots are made in Geelong and South Gippsland. Bannockburn, By Farr and Scotchmans Hill have made a name for themselves but the wine that every Pinot enthusiast craves is Bass Phillip's Reserve Pinot, one of Australia's most exceptional wines made by Phillip Jones. I have yet to taste this quartet of Pinots but hope for that pleasure in the near future.

Pinot Noir is probably the longest established of the main red varieties. It was most decisively developed by Cistercian monks at Burgundy's Clos de Vougeot, following an empirical approach. They observed, analysed and studied each component of terroir – microclimate, soil and grape variety – and their diligent and perceptive husbandry raised viticulture to an agronomic art form as they constantly refined their techniques. The most prized Burgundy still comes from the walled plots that they identified hundreds of years ago, plots in well drained mid-slope sites where there is excellent exposure to sun and warmth from early morning.

The Valois Dukes of Burgundy, led by Philip the Bold, were quick to learn the advantages of public relations. Having secured the endorsement of the French Court at Versailles they promoted Burgundy as 'the best wine in the world.'

Mornington Peninsula is an enterprising region that organizes an annual International Pinot Noir celebration inviting Pinot Noir producers from around the world to taste and compare great Pinots from Burgundy, California, Oregon, Ontario, South Africa, New Zealand, Chile as well as the other Pinot Noir producing regions of Australia. It is also an excellent opportunity to show off the richness of the local food supply which has encouraged many top chefs to move out from Melbourne.

However, despite the progress that Pinot Noir has been making in prime sites around Melbourne, there is a more general feeling that the variety has not reached its full potential in Australia. Indeed, one group of wine enthusiasts, considered the wines so unexceptional that they formed the 'Australian Pinot Noir-Why do We Bother? Society.'

This reaction may well have developed because there was a general tendency for larger Australian growers to consider all Pinot Noir clones as being more or less the same. For a long time such growers relied on such standard clones as the Burgundian MW6 and the high yielding Californian UC Davis clones, neither of which generate much intensity of fruit flavour, nor do they impart much elegance or finesse to the wines.

The more specialist Australian Pinot Noir growers tried and tested a whole range of Dijon clones and selected 114, 115, 292, 386, 667 and 777 as the most satisfactory. They also retained the best of the UC Davis clones. Over the last 20 years or so these clones have become conditioned to the Australian environment and are coming to maturity. Those more determined growers who made the long trek up to Burgundy to select their clonal material and learn about such Burgundian practices as close-planting (to encourage vine roots to push deeper), cold soaking, and whole bunch fermentation to develop fresh fruit flavours, have mostly benefited from the time and expense by producing fine wines saleable at higher prices.

However, the truth is that great Pinot Noir will always be difficult to produce in large quantities because it is made from low yielding vines which give better texture, more intensity of flavour and greater longevity.

The foregoing suggests that, as far as Australian Pinot Noir is concerned, enthusiasts will probably do better to follow winemakers, such as those I have mentioned in Victoria and the Adelaide Hills, or will mention in Tasmania, rather the than the regions themselves. I venture to suggest that Victoria is probably better blessed with climatic conditions and soils and certainly has a greater number of top notch producers.

176

Pinot Noir ready for harvesting

TASMANIA

When I first entered the wine trade Tasmania did not raise even the faintest blip on the wine radar screen. Situated in the southern ocean, 150 miles south of the mainland, it was known, if at all, as the wet and windy home of the Tasmanian Devil, a smelly, carnivorous marsupial with a stronger bite than any other living mammal. If the capital Hobart registered in my mind it was only as the finishing point for one of the world's toughest ocean yacht races.

Fifty years on, Tasmania is one of the 'hot' spots of Australian viticulture recognised for the excellence of its sparkling wine and the promise of its Pinot Noir. Ironically, it is a 'hot' spot because of its cool climate. An island in an ocean, its hottest days are kept in check by sea breezes with western mountains to protect inland valleys from any stronger winds. Cool nights and long, mild autumns encourage the development of fruit flavours. The small yields (compared with Champagne) mean greater concentration of flavours.

Old sandstone soils washed with the sediments of marine life and later   subject to volcanic activity, provide rich mineral soils from which the vines derive their good health. The natural acidity of the soil yields the high acid musts essential for the production of top quality sparkling wine.

As the current cycle of global warming makes warm climate vineyards even warmer the level of natural acidity in grapes starts to fall. Extra warmth means higher sugar content in the grapes which translates into higher levels of alcohol. Too much heat also causes reduction in fruit flavour and can have an adverse effect on the balance of wines. Higher levels of carbon dioxide means more leaf than fruit growth producing 'green' (slightly bitter, unripe flavours) wines that consumers do not appreciate. Heat also contributes to vine stress (particularly to fragrant white varieties) increasing the need for irrigation: it also encourages more active insect life, some of which is harmful. All the above makes Tasmania a very attractive region for producing top quality for cool climate wines.

Dr Andrew Pirie, the first Australian to earn a PhD in Viticulture, was the first modern

winemaker to really appreciate Tasmania's potential for producing the classic cool climate varieties. Pirie's definition of 'cool' means an average growing season temperature of 19C or 1150 day degrees, the same as Champagne, Chablis, Burgundy, the Rhine and Mosel. In the southern hemisphere, only Marlborough and Central Otago in New Zealand, and the higher hills around Adelaide and Melbourne combine great terroir with such cool conditions.

Pinot Noir and Chardonnay are the two most important varieties grown in Tasmania accounting for 70% of plantings: Riesling, Sauvignon Blanc and Pinot Gris make up most of the rest.

Pinot Noir (70% of red grape plantings) performs well in Tasmania, particularly in the warmer south where the newer Dijon clones have been matched with appropriate soils and

180

microclimates as in the Coal River Valley area and more sheltered sites on the east coast. Carefully selected warm spots within these cooler climates produce Pinot Noirs with delicate aromas and pure fruit flavours.

As we have seen on the mainland if the weather gets too warm, heat stifles natural fruit flavours. In Tasmania the soil and climatic conditions encourage natural acidity which in turn enhances fruit flavour. Furthermore, lower yields mean more concentrated flavours. Fermentation and maturation techniques also contribute to a leaner and more aromatic style of wine.

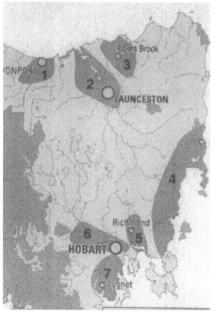

Tasmania is a very small region with only 1400 hectares of vineyard producing an average of 9600 tonnes of fruit, about 1% of the total Australian crush! However, it is important to bear in mind that her entire focus is on producing quality wines for which there is an established demand.

The Tasmanian wine industry is comprised of a few large companies producing sparkling wine and around 200 small family wineries producing table wines.

The largest sparkling wine producers are in the areas around Launceston and Pipers Brook region (1, 2 and 3 on the map) while the top table wine producers are in the river valleys around Hobart (5, 6 and 7). The other significant wine producing area is on the east coast (4) around Bichero where excellent sparkling and both red and white varietal wines are produced. Tasmania's main claim to fame is the quality of its sparkling wines and Pinot Noirs. The focus on quality suits those gifted winemakers that have come here with high ideals and the courage to explore their own ideas about making great wines. Without the distractions of the mainland they can quietly work in a pristine environment. The weather may not always be as kind as they would like but the expectation is that there will be gradual warming that may encourage planting of a wider range of varieties. In the meantime, when the sun shines and the wind drops, the grapes are blessed with favourable conditions.

PIPERS BROOK

The Pipers Brook Estate, established in 1974 by Dr Andrew Pirie, was acquired by  Kreglinger, the Belgian wool merchants, in 2001. Kreglinger initiated its Australian wine interests with the development of the Norfolk Rise estate in the Mount Benson area of South Australia.

The Pipers Brook region is considered to be one of the finest sites for sparkling wine outside Champagne. In fact Champagne Louis Roederer was one of the first foreign companies to invest in the region although it later sold its vineyards to Pipers Brook and its Jansz brand name to Yalumba.

It is thought that Roederer ran out of patience with the Tasmanian climate because in the 1980s the Pinot Noir resolutely refused to ripen. A decade or so later the climate seems to have improved and better clonal material has been planted in more sheltered, warmer sites. The Pinot ripens better and the wines are fuller-bodied.

Kreglinger inherited fine and beautifully maintained vineyards which have been further improved and expanded. The winery has been updated with more modern disgorging equipment and a new dosage regime introduced. The Kreglinger sparkling wine range includes Brut, Blanc de Blanc and Rosé all of which are stylishly packaged for both the domestic and export markets.

The winery also produces a range of table wines under the Pipers Brook and Nine Islands names. The 2005 Lyre Pinot Noir Reserve stood out from other wines and shows just how well the variety can perform when the cultivar is planted in more sheltered and warmer sites. The Riesling and Chardonnay varietal wines are also made to a high standard and are competitively priced. The Ninth Island range includes both Pinot Grigio and Sauvignon Blanc.

CLOVER HILL

Taltarni Vineyards, established in Victoria's Pyrenees region in 1972, has always aspired to make fine sparkling wine. In 1986 the company acquired the 66 hectare Clovers Hill estate in the Pipers Brook area of north-east Tasmania because of the similarity of its soils and climate to the Champagne region of France. It later acquired the 44 hectare Lalla Gully Estate to the east of Launceston where it produces aromatic Riesling, Chardonnay, Sauvignon Blanc, Pinot Gris and Pinot Noir under the Lalla Gully label.

Clover Hill has planted Chardonnay, Pinot Noir and Pinot Meunier on an open hillside overlooking the Bass Strait which we visited on a warm and balmy day. What made it better was the greeting with a glass of Clover Hill Blanc de Blanc, one of the best Tasmanian sparkling wines. I admired the fragrant, floral style, creamy flavour and fine persistent mousse. Winemaker Loic Le Calvez is rightly proud her wines that are increasingly popular on the mainland.

Lalla Gully wines revealed the vibrant acidity and purity of fruit flavour that we have come to expect even after a few short days in Tasmania!

BAY OF FIRES

Bay of Fires, owned by Constellation Wines, is a 23 hectare estate established in 2001, to produce premium sparkling wines on the recommendation of Ed Carr, the group's senior sparkling winemaker, recognized as one of the best in Australia.

Another of Carr's inspired decisions was to appoint Fran Austin winemaker at Bay of Fives. She has turned out to be one of the industry's brightest stars and the Bay of Fires wines have proved so successful that the company now buys in grapes from 17 contracted growers, spread across the island.

Fran Austin's skills derive from her ability to identify the best parcels of grapes and to nurse them through to maturity. We tasted her 2001 Blanc de Blanc, specially disgorged for us to taste, because the wine will stay on its lees until 2011. Rich and generously flavoured it was wonderfully pure and clean on the palate. After we had tasted the wine and commented on it, Fran admitted that it had been made from an exceptional parcel of grapes, and that she was constantly on the lookout for similar parcels. It is that kind of skill, understanding and dedication that makes winemaking so interesting and so special. The tasting included other vintages of Arras (including the 1998 released in 2009) which showed how these extremely classy wines benefit from long leas contact. Austin's winemaking is marvellously consistent. It begins with the careful selection of fruit and ends with poised and elegant finished wines that are a joy to drink.

TAMAR RIDGE

The Tamar Ridge Estate, now owned by Brown Brothers who have 700 hectares in Victoria and the Hunter Valley, comprises 200 hectares in 4 different locations. Dr Andrew Pirie, CEO and Chief Winemaker at the time of our visit, stressed that in laying out the estate his key consideration was how he could produce the highest quality grapes. 'Quality is vital to the future of the Tasmanian wine industry. At Tamar Ridge we concentrated on identifying our best terroirs, matching clones to them, and developing cool climate viticultural techniques to get the very best out of them.'

To illustrate his point Dr Pirie explained that by carefully selecting warmer sites for the selected Dijon Pinot Noir clones, he had been able to make Reserve class wines only four years after planting.

Dr Pirie's commitment to viticultural research and development was made apparent when he retained the services of Dr Richard Smart, one of the world's leading viticultural consultants, to oversee the planning of the varietal planting programme and the development of the appropriate viticultural practices. The Kayena vineyard is superbly organised and produces superb grapes from several different varieties.

Already famous for his work on canopy management designed to increase air flow around vines, and grape exposure to the sun, Dr Smart also co-ordinates Tamar Ridge's own research programme, largely directed at protecting the natural soil structure with soil nutrients, fertigation (the delivery of soluble nutrients timed to plant growth cycles) and the testing of organic soil additives and the use of mulching to increase organic matter.

Smart also takes a particular interest in pest management. As the current global warming cycle develops he anticipates the proliferation of vine diseases and unwanted pests such as the light brown apple-moth.

Smart has also directed important research work with the Tasmanian Institute of Agricultural Research and PhD students from the University of Tasmania at the Tamar Ridge micro-vinification facilities. There are a number of on-going projects but the most important is focused on quality improvements in Pinot Noir, which accounts for over 40% of plantings in Tasmania.

I was intrigued and impressed by his clonal trials. There are a total of 23 Pinot Noir clones on trial but Smart selected six micro-vinifications for us to taste, including one from the 'relic collection' thought to have been brought to Australia in 1832 by James Busby, two Burgundian clones, another of French

(Pommard) origin developed at University of California Davis, and one from the Hunter Valley. The variances were subtle and it was intriguing trying to work out which was which. However, it was an extremely worthwhile diversion because we were able to understand the objectives of the research and evaluate the progress that is being made in a field so important to the future of Tasmanian grape growing.

The four different Tamar Ridge vineyard locations Estate are 135 hectares at Kayena in the Tamar Valley (pictured above), 167 hectares at Coombend on the east coast, 83 hectares at White Hills and three hectares at Rosevears.

Kayena is home to the modern state-of-the-art winery where the whole range of wines including Devils Corner, Notley Gorge and Pirie are produced to a very high standard. The most memorable wine was 2007 Kayena Sauvignon Blanc which for its sublime purity of fruit.

JANSZ TASMANIA

When Champagne Louis Roederer decided to withdraw from Tasmania in 1986 they sold some of their land to Yalumba together with the Jansz brand name. Yalumba has since expanded the vineyards and the winery and in so doing completely revitalized the business.

Natalie Fryar, the winemaker at Jansz, is another of the highly talented lady winemakers who oversee production of the islands finest sparkling wines. Trained at Seppelts in Great Western Victoria Fryar spends a lot of her time walking the vineyards, 'getting to know the fruit' as she puts it.

Of the Jansz wines tasted the Jansz Premium Vintage Cuvee 2005 rated most highly. Made with more or less an even split of Chardonnay and Pinot Noir the wine spent five years on the lees building texture and complexity before its release.

Jansz is a modern winery with a superb tasting room appropriately called the Wine Room where enthusiasts can explore the whole Jansz range at their leisure, comparing different styles and vintages, and learning about the grapes grown, their vineyard management and winery processing. Jansz designed the Wine Room as an interpretive centre to help visitors understand why the soil and climatic conditions in Tasmania produce some of the world's very best sparkling wines.

MOORILLA ESTATE

The Estate was founded by Claudio Alcorso, an Italian industrial designer who immigrated to Tasmania in 1937 and was the first significant wine property to be established in Tasmania. Since 1996 Moorilla has been owned by David Walsh, a successful businessman who plans to open the Museum of Old and New Art (MONA) at Moorilla in 2011. His purpose is to attract prime target visitors to the island and his winery.

MONA will be the largest privately funded museum in Australia but it is only one of a number of attractions planned for visitors to the winery. There is a huge outdoor stage for concerts and other entertainments, a conference suite with restaurants, luxurious waterside cabin accommodation for holiday rentals and a superb micro brewery producing the famous Moo Brew beers. According to Daniel McMahon, Moorilla's Cellar Door Manager, wine tourism will play a big part in the winery's business and in attracting visitors to the island.

Conor van der Reest, the winemaker at Moorilla is a cool climate specialist from Ontario Canada, whose well-made, aromatic and slender Sauvignon Blanc, Riesling and Chardonnay wines all show lively acids: the Gewurztraminer was pleasantly spicy. The winery has a good record of producing quality Pinot Noir while the Cabernet blends gain richness from 12 months maturation in wood.

The Cloth Label series includes a stylish cool climate Syrah and a Pinot Noir made from low yielding Dijon clones with delicate and delightful fruit flavours and noticeably lower-than-normal alcohol levels, a wine which owed a great deal to precise viticultural treatment.

Having completed the wine tasting we really enjoyed our visit to Moorilla's micro brewery and its freshly brewed and immensely popular Moo brew.

STEFANO LUBIANA

On arrival at the small family winery on the Derwent River, 15 miles north of Hobart there was no sign of Stefano Lubiana. However, a strong whiff of fishbone manure wafting across the premises suggested that he was not too far away fertilizing his soil - a salient reminder that the Tasmanian wine industry is mainly made up of small, dedicated family businesses in which the owner(s) has to turn his/her hand to a wide variety of tasks.

The Lubiana family, originally from Trieste, settled in the Barossa but in 1989 Stefano left the relative comfort of the family business to come to Tasmania 'to make a more varied and more interesting range of wines.' He found an ideal cool climate site with well drained soils in a protected little valley overlooking the tidal estuary of the Derwent and planted his 18 hectares with Chardonnay and Pinot Noir, also finding space for Riesling, Pinot Gris, Sauvignon Blanc, Merlot and the Cabernets! Lubiana relishes the opportunity to make different varietal wines because, he says, it helps him learn more about his land and what he likes doing best – producing small quantities of hand crafted wines that push back the boundaries of winemaking and exploring innovative methods of extracting the maximum amount of aroma and fruit flavour.

He offered a medley of flavours to taste starting with a fresh, crisp Riesling suitably named Alfresco, followed by a fresh Sauvignon Blanc, a fruity Chardonnay and a fascinating Pinot Gris Vin Santo.

His two premium sparkling wines bottled under the Prestige label revealed just why Tasmanian fizz is so highly regarded the 1995 was rich, generous taste and buttery – outstanding wine at the top of its form. Over a memorable farmhouse lunch, prepared by his wife Monique, we enjoyed a classy, well-structured, richly robed 2005 Pinot Noir Sasso

made from Dijon clones planted soon after his arrival and coming to maturity.

Lubiana is clearly a gifted vigneron worth following whatever he produces: he is a good example of the modern Australian winemaker, a talented vintner with the self belief required to sink all available capital into a project that will not yield a financial return for many years. Together with those other Tasmanian winemakers we visited and the likes of Claudio Radenti at Freycinet and Brian Fanklin at Apsley Gorge, they have raised the profile of Tasmanian wines and merit inclusion in your itinerary when you come Down Under, or when you have a chance to taste their wines.

DOMAINE A

Peter Althaus trained as an engineer but spent most of his career running the IBM office in Switzerland. However, at the age of 49, an opportunity arose for him to indulge his long held ambition and desire to make his own wines – in the southern Hemisphere.

He set off for South America and Australasia looking for cool climate conditions similar to those of his preferred European wine areas. Time spent in reconnaissance is rarely wasted and having looked at several potential sites across both continents he found what he was looking for at Stoney vineyard in the Coal River Valley, 30 minutes drive north of Hobart in Tasmania. However, the vineyard was not for sale. Undaunted he secured the first option to buy it, if and when the owner decided to move on. The purchase was completed in 1996 since when the estate has been extended to 20 hectares mostly close planted with the Cabernets, Merlot, Petit Verdot and Pinot Noir, and a little Sauvignon Blanc.

As befits an engineer Althaus does everything with great precision. He knows exactly what he wants from his vines and works tirelessly in both vineyard and cellar to achieve his aims. Pruning, shoot positioning, leaf removal, and harvesting are done by hand and he personally selects all the fruit that to be processed. He has invested in the very best equipment he can find to do what he has always dreamt of doing, making individual wines in accordance with his own ideas. The first wine tasted, a steely, dry Sauvignon Blanc showed him to be a very thorough and classy winemaker.

The Cabernet Sauvignon and Merlot wines were so rich in flavour that it was hard to believe they had been made on such a wet and windy island. Althaus explained that he had planted them in the warmest, most sheltered sites he could find on his land and that with careful viticulture and fine summer weather and a long sunny autumn the grapes gently ripened to the desired level.

Many commentators consider that Australia is simply too hot for making the concentrated, balanced, silky-textured Merlots for which Bordeaux's right bank has become famous and yet Althaus manages to achieve phenolic ripeness without excessive alcohol.

His 2004 Cabernet Sauvignon is one of the best cabernet blends that I have tasted in Australia, finely structured, rich and complete with a long finish and a tribute to his patient husbandry.

Domaine A wines are worth seeking out as examples of Tasmania's very top red wines, made without compromise from low yields from meticulously maintained vineyards. The more competitively priced Stoney Vineyard label has rightly earned a reputation for its excellent value for money.

PIRIE TASMANIA

In addition to making wine at Tamar Ridge Dr Andrew Pirie's own company Pirie Tasmania distributes wines that he makes under the brand names Pirie Estate, Pirie Reserve and South.

South Chardonnay and Pinot Noir, which have recently been stylishly repackaged, are excellent examples of the clean, clear, fruit led cool climate wines of the region just to the south of Launceston produced without oak.

Pirie Estate wines are made from low yields of selected fruit from specific blocks considered to be above average: they are managed to ensure higher than average quality of fruit and are models of their type. The 2005 Pinot Noir that I tasted had an aromatic cherry fruit nose and lovely pure fruit expression. Pirie Reserve wines, only produced in exceptional years when the grapes are absolutely perfect, reveal all the care and attention to detail for which Andrew Pirie has become recognized. These are superb examples of their type and I particularly admired the Chardonnay.

Pirie Sparkling is not only recognized as one of the very best sparkling wines produced on the island, but considered by such renowned international sparkling wine commentators as Tom Stevenson, to be one of the finest sparkling wines in the world, made to the same standard as good Champagne.

Andrew Pirie's success is thoroughly deserved. Since he first came to Tasmania when preparing his PhD and recognized its potential for Chardonnay and Pinot Noir (its climate is very similar to Burgundy) he has devoted his career to putting Tasmanian wines on the wine map of the world. In so doing he has worked alongside the Tasmanian wine authorities to establish fine wine viticulture, being instrumental in shaping two large scale vineyards – Pipers Brook and Tamar Ridge – as well as developing his own more modestly sized one. He is a winemaker that one can absolutely trust to produce sound, attractive table wines and outstanding sparkling wines.

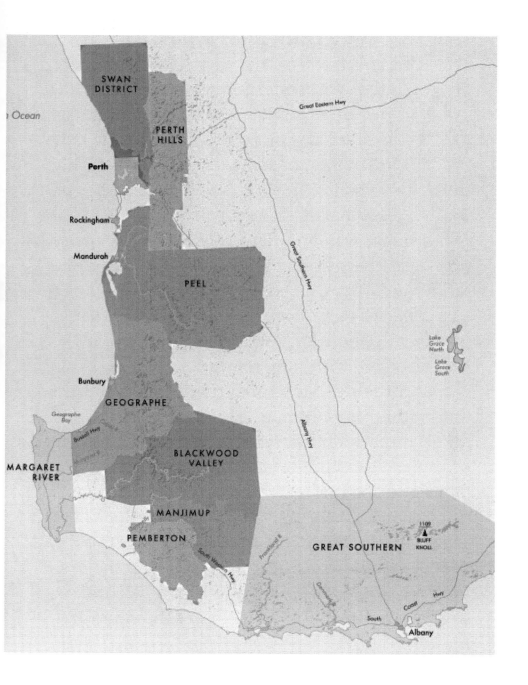

Wine Regions of Western Australia

WESTERN AUSTRALIA

Although Western Australia, with 4000 hectares under vine only produces around 5% of Australia's wine, it now is home to some of its most highly rated vineyards. The first plantations in the Swan Valley north of Perth produced wine in 1834, but it was another 100 years before they produced their first really successful dry white table wine from Chenin Blanc.

The move to cooler climates in the Great Southern region around Mount Barker (not to be confused with the mountain of the same name in the Adelaide Hills) accelerated interest and viticulture spread to nearby Frankland and Denmark on the south coast.

However, the real turning point in the fame and fortune of the West Australian wine trade came with the 1965 publication of a report by the State's chief agronomist, Dr John Gladstones in which he suggested that the area between Cape Leeuwin and Cape Naturaliste was a good place to plant vines but the area around Willyabrup near the small inland township of Margaret River was ideal because the soils were friable and the vineyards would be favourably influenced by the warmer winds of the Indian Ocean, rather than the colder Antarctic winds of the southern Ocean.

Three doctors, all hobby winemakers, read the report and acted on its findings. Kevin Cullen, Tom Cullity and Bill Pannell all bought small plots near Willyabrup and planted Chardonnay and Cabernet Sauvignon. The first results were so promising that they planted more land and established family companies - Cullen, Vasse Felix and Moss Wood respectively. Other vintners soon noted the quality of the wines they were producing and several bought plots to develop, notably David and Mark Hohnen at Cape Mentelle.

Gladstone's report, published in the Journal of the Australian Institute of Agricultural Science, became a 'best-seller' in the wine trade and five editions were printed. Growers, winemakers and investors rushed to Margaret River to evaluate the opportunity for themselves. They experienced the warm, balmy climate mentioned in the report and the gentle breezes it promised. Sea breezes are essential to grape growing in such a warm climate but if vineyards are too close to the ocean stronger winds - more gales than breezes- can cause damage and retard ripening. Soil analysis confirmed the presence of the very minerals to support healthy vines.

It seems unfair that a region that arrived so late on the scene, and which is so modest in terms of production, should have caught the interest and imagination of the wine public so quickly. But there is no doubt whatsoever that Dr Gladstone's recommendation was spot on: Margaret River's well drained ridge of iron rich clay is a very suitable region for growing Cabernet Sauvignon and quite a few other varieties as well.

However, before claiming it as a perfect site we should take into account the local flora and fauna. The area is rich in gum trees that have attracted a huge kangaroo population for whom early budding shoots are delicious nourishment. And the lime green parrots that patrol the place have a vested interest in being on hand when the grapes ripen. Thus netting and bird scarers go with the territory. Another problem is the modest rainfall- just 1160mm in the year making irrigation essential. Despite these problems the conditions are superb for growing grapes in a stress free environment with the acid and tannin structure that adds intensity to their natural fruit flavours.

CULLEN

Margaret River wines ooze class and finesse, none more so than Vanya Cullen's Diana Madeleine, named for her late mother, a founding partner in the estate with her husband. It is a breathtaking blend of Cabernet Sauvignon with Merlot, made from 100% biodynamically grown grapes. Cullen claims that biodynamic farming helps black grapes achieve phenolic ripeness at lower sugar levels, which means lower alcohol levels, and produces wines with greater vitality. Moreover her soils remain healthy and her wines live longer.

Her other flagship wine is Kevin John Chardonnay, selected by Decanter as the best Chardonnay of 2009. It is a superb example of Margaret River Chardonnay. The Decanter Award entries (from all over the world) are tasted blind. The Trophy wines are assessed by three different panels, and it is a considerable achievement to come out top after such a demanding process.

Cullen's Sauvignon Blanc-Semillon blend has also been highly praised but she modestly deflects personal praise, preferring that it is given to the run of near perfect recent vintages. When pushed for a preference she nominates her favourite as what she calls the Mozart vintage of 2009 – because both the red and white wines achieved wonderful harmony.

The Mangan vineyard is planted to Sauvignon Blanc and Semillon, and also has some Petit Verdot, Merlot and Malbec. Cullen Malbec has considerable potential and may turn out to be more interesting than Merlot. Cullen is one of the outstanding vineyards of the region and its wines are some of the most sought after in Australia.

VASSE FELIX

Dr Tom Cullit planted his first vines in 1967 and slowly expanded the Vasse Felix Estate while building its reputation for producing fine wines. It was subsequently acquired by the Holmes à Court family which, on hearing that the vineyards were for sale, made an immediate offer to buy and completed the purchase in 1987.

Paul Holmes à Court considers himself to be the fortunate custodian of a wonderful terroir. The family has considerably expanded and modernized the estate always with a view to enhancing the quality of its wines. Renowned for its Chardonnay and Cabernet Sauvignon Vasse Felix has increased its range to include a very stylish Semillon-Sauvignon Blanc blend.

Virginia Willcock, the Chief Winemaker, praises the abundant sunshine that provides the warmth that makes the vines so healthy. She also blesses the late afternoon breezes

which keep them stress free. Most of the older vines are now around 35 years old and produce small berried grapes perfect for winemaking. She modestly implies that all she has to do in the winery is to stick her nose in the vats to tell her when the wine is ready.

The Holmes à Courts have made Vasse Felix a delightfully stylish winery to visit. Entry is through a unique underground cellar and after tasting, lunch can be taken in a spectacular restaurant before visiting the high class exhibition of paintings in the Art gallery.

MOSS WOOD

Even though Bill Pannell (father of Steve in McLaren Vale) read Dr John Gladstone's report on wine production in south western Australia he still searched for six months before he found the site he wanted to plant his vineyard in Margaret River. His first vintage - all Cabernet Sauvignon - was made in 1972 and Moss Wood Cabernets have been consistently good ever since. In 1976 he planned to plant Chardonnay but since there were no top quality clones available, he chose Semillon instead. He eventually planted the desired

Chardonnay clones and it is these three varieties which have become the winery's specialities.

Dr Pannell chose Keith Mugford as winemaker. It was the start of his long association with the estate that he and his wife acquired from the Pannells in 1985. They have four children and have been very considerate in acquiring the Ribbon Vale vineyard to expand the business sufficiently to allow room for all four children to take part should they wish to do so.

Cabernet Sauvignon, Chardonnay and a seductive Semillon are the house specialties. I tasted the 2001 and 2005 Cabernet wines which were of the highest class and confirm Dr Pannell's wisdom in taking note of the Gladstone's report and choosing his site so carefully.

CAPE MENTELLE

The vineyards, carefully planted in an east-west orientation two miles inland, quickly established their pedigree, and the Hohnen brothers produced breathtaking white and red wines. The aromatic, fresh juicy blend of

Sauvignon Blanc- Semillon won immediate attention and approval. As a result of their success, David, exploring New Zealand, found a a wonderful site for growing Sauvignon Blanc at Marlborough. It

The phenomenal success of Cloudy Bay is another story, but it led to an offer for 50% of the Hohnen business from Champagne Veuve Cliquot. When Cliquot was acquired by luxury goods manufacturer LVMH it took complete control in 2002.

The new owners have extended Cape Mentelle which now has four regional vineyards and some 200 hectares under vine. It is good to report that the quality of the wines has developed at the same time. The Cabernet Sauvignon for instance, has evolved into a luscious, full-bodied, plush wine with pronounced blackberry and mulberry flavours. The secret is the wonderful site and low yields of around eight tonnes per hectare. The 2008 Sauvignon Blanc-Semillon and Chardonnay are as good as anything I have tasted from Western Australia.

The current senior winemaker is Robert Mann, grandson of the legendary winemaker Jack Mann MBE who made so many fine wines at Houghton Winery in the Swan valley from 1930-1974. Mann is positive that the regional climate, clarity of fruit and subtle West Australian nuances will distinguish his Shiraz from those of other regions.

LEEUWIN ESTATE

Of all the new start-ups in the Margaret River region, the one that intrigues me most is Leeuwin Estate. Denis Horgan, a successful merchant banker in Perth, loved surfing on the huge waves east of the Margaret River township and decided to buy a plumbing business there. With the plumbing business came a parcel of land south of the river with which he did nothing. Until he got a telephone call from a Seattle based lawyer enquiring about the possibility of purchasing the land.

It transpired from Horgan's enquiries that the interested party was the Californian winemaker Robert Mondavi who was convinced that the region was ideal for the production of Chardonnay. Horgan decided to keep the land but co-opted Mondavi as his mentor and advisor. Mondavi advised on the establishment of a nursery to supply the pedigree vine stock required to make fine wine.

The Chardonnay produced in 1980 was so good that it was picked out by a highly qualified Decanter Award judging panel as being exceptional and all the world's wine critics seem to agree that the Leeuwin Art Series Chardonnay has become a benchmark for Australian Chardonnay.

Richly textured, complex, savoury and long lasting it is a wine that has represented Australia around the world and it can stand up

proudly in any Chardonnay company.

There are now four other superb wines in the Art Series range: Cabernet Sauvignon, Shiraz, Sauvignon Blanc and Riesling. These are opulent wines quite beautifully made and presented. They are supported by Prelude Chardonnay and Cabernet Sauvignon which are also made to a very high standard. The Sibling range is produced from younger vines and is generally ready to drink a little earlier than Art Series and Prelude wines.

Leeuwin has also become famous for the great annual concerts that it has staged every year since 1983. Dame Kiri de Kanawa, Ray Charles and Tom Jones are some of the all-time greats who have performed at Leeuwin Concerts which were, of course, started to attract attention to the wines.

The Horgans have an innate sense of style and not only produce great wine but also provide a gracious ambiance in which to enjoy it. To think that Leeuwin started with the purchase of a plumbing business close to the Indian Ocean that had attracted the attention of a Californian wine producer.

XANADU

Samuel Taylor Coleridge was known to appreciate other substances than wine but his Kubla Khan poem, based on a vision of a stately pleasure garden called Xanadu, caught the imagination of Dr John Langan when he named his new vineyard in Margaret River. He had arrived from Belfast in 1968 just as three local medics were busy planting small trial vineyards in their spare time. It took him a few more years to get going but the result was some spectacular Chardonnay.

After he retired and sold the vineyard it went through a difficult period and it was not until it was acquired by the Rathbone family in 2005 that it took a decided turn for the better.

The Rathbone family owns three other superb properties, Yering Station in the Yarra Valley, Parker Coonawarra Estate and Mount Langi Ghiran in the Grampian mountains. Darren Rathbone is the director in charge of winemaking and he has been the driving force in the decision to focus on producing top quality wines at each estate.

Xanadu was completely overhauled and enlarged to 85 hectares. The emphasis remains on Chardonnay and Cabernet Sauvignon, but Semillon and Sauvignon Blanc have been added to the portfolio. I tasted their 2008 and 2009 Estate and Reserve wines at the Australia Day tasting in London and was delighted to find both wines back to their best.

VOYAGER ESTATE

The naming of this estate also has an interesting story behind it. When Michael Wright bought the property in 1991 he wanted to find ways of attracting visitors to this remote corner of Western Australia. Of Scottish ancestry his interest in history led him to explore the influences on the development of Australia.

The Dutch, who dominated the merchant marine in the seventeenth century, encouraged their traders to open new markets. That brought the first mariners to the region and in 1602 the Dutch East India Company was formed to exercise its monopoly of trade east of the Cape of Good Hope. For 200 years the Company traded the spices, teas, silks and porcelain that were so desirable to European ruling classes. The Company was dissolved in 1800 but the Wright family acquired the rights to its logo which they incorporated into the logo of their successful iron ore business.

Thus when the winery was built the South African Cape Dutch style was chosen. However, Wrights ambition was to make great wine and he started by securing excellent land in the Stevens Valley where the maritime climate and well drained gravel soils encouraged the growth of healthy vines.

In many wineries the winemaker is heralded as the hero. At Voyager Estate head viticulturalist is revered. Not that he lets it go to his head. He likes to keep things simple in the vineyard, applying sound viticultural practice to the production of top quality fruit. John Bernard Delmas, the legendary Director of wine at Bordeaux's Chateau Haut Brion believes 'that by the time the grapes reach the winery, the wine is made.'

In recent years the emphasis of the viticultural work has been developing the clonal selection of new plantings and using organic methods where ever possible to generate bacterial life in the soils.

Chardonnay and Cabernet Sauvignon dominate the plantings but there is also Sauvignon Blanc, Semillon, Petit Verdot, Malbec and Chenin Blanc.

The Chardonnay has great charm and enormous appeal with its stone-fruit flavours and creamy nuttiness that comes from regular lees stirring. The grapes are picked early to retain freshness, wild yeasts are used to stimulate fermentation and oak is discreetly used to add texture and tone. Altogether this is a sophisticated, sensibly-priced fine wine. The 2004 Voyager Estate Cabernet Sauvignon-Merlot blend is also a very accomplished wine – elegant, complex and beautifully balanced.

The Cellar Door facilities are also superb comprising a first class restaurant, landscaped gardens from which one can see the meticulously maintained vineyards and impressive underground cellars in which to mature the finest wines.

HOWARD PARK

Howard Park is another of the great wine families of Australia which was established in the Great Southern region of Western Australia in 1986 when founder John Wade came because he believed he could make both great Rieslings and Cabernet Sauvignons there. Having done that he bought land around Margaret River and the business is now run by Jeff and Amy Burch. They have made an uncompromising commitment to produce the best possible grapes and David Botting their chief viticulturalist overseas the vineyards while Janice McDonald has recently taken over the mantle of senior winemaker.

The vineyards were extended with the purchase of Leston Hill in 2000 and the new winery built in the middle of the vineyard on top of the hill with commanding views over Willyabrup. The winery has been given a five star rating by the ever vigilant James Halliday and its flagship Abercrombie range is produced from superb fruit. The 2008 Cabernet Sauvignon is highly prized for its all round excellence.

Jeff Burch has developed a special relationship with Burgundian grower Pascal Marchand who makes wine for Comte Armand in Pommard's Premier Cru vineyard Clos des Epeneaux. Both men, close friends, wanted to try to create a collection of enjoyable wines under screwcap that express their ideas about what day-to-day and special occasion wines can be like when two different but complimentary experiences are applied.

PIERRO

The name Pierro is a play on Peterkin. Dr Mike Peterkin is yet another of the medical profession who has turned his fulltime attention to making fine wine. Without beating about the bush, Peterkin is a wizard with Chardonnay, but all his wines are made with extraordinary care and attention to detail.

Perhaps because I first learned about Chardonnay in Burgundy I have always had a preference for concentrated, multi-flavoured, creamy, nutty wines. In Australia there are so many delicious variations of that theme. Peterkin seems to be a man put on this earth to make sublime Burgundian styled Chardonnay. His biggest advantage over Burgundy is the climate. Peterkin considers that Margaret River must be one of the best places on earth to make wine because of its predictable warm climate cooled by ocean breezes which keeps vines so healthy and happy. Its well drained, old mineral soils allow deep root penetration. He uses such advantages to produce a full-bodied and fruity Chardonnays made more interesting by malolactic fermentation, lees stirring and maturation in new French oak.

His main intervention is in the choice of sites, clonal selection and in higher density plantings. He is a disciple of Richard Smart nd pays a great deal of attention to canopy management.

He also accepts the role of controlled irrigation in the vineyard (just as refrigeration is used in the modern winery) and follows organic practices wherever possible.

Peterkin's ability to assess situations and to think through viticultural problems in terms of his own property is uncanny. For example he worked out that on his land he could get 20% more sunlight by orienting his vines north south rather than east-west. He also worked out that his vines would be more productive if they were close planted at around 5000 vines per hectare than the conventional Australian 1900 per hectare. He maintains, and it shows in his wines, that good balance and flavour intensity are enhanced by close planting. He is the kind of winemaker that I trust and am inclined to follow because I sense that the pursuit of excellence is his raison d'être.

Apart from his sublime Chardonnay I also admired his Cabernet Sauvignon/Merlot LTCF blend. For those of you as mystified as I was by the LTCF moniker it means Little Touch of Cabernet Franc. Actually in the 2008 there is 11% Cabernet Franc in the blend and a little touch -2%- of Petit Verdot! This blend is made by fermenting some of the wine on its skins and then giving it extended skin contact; most of the wine is fermented in open top tanks with just a few days skin contact, the balance in closed fermentation vessels. The wine is then racked into French oak for 12 months maturation. Each to his own but this winemaker, who I have never met, enthrals me with all his wines.

OTHER WEST AUSTRALIAN WINERIES

The West Australian wine industry largely developed in the Swan Valley, 300 miles north of Margaret River. Houghton Wines is often an underestimated label simply because it is not in the Margaret River region but I commend you to try Houghton White Show Reserve, a blend of many white varieties but mostly Chardonnay, Chenin Blanc and Semillon.

Houghton will also surprise you with the quality of its Reserve Chardonnay and the super premium Cabernet Sauvignon named for its celebrated former winemaker Jack Mann whose grandson Robert is now winemaker at Cape Mentelle. More recently Houghton has introduced The Bandit series, inspired by the bushranger Moondyne Joe, who mounted an audacious bid to steal the new harvest wines in 1869. The Bandit blends are equally daring-Sauvignon Blanc with Pinot Gris: Chardonnay with Viognier: and Shiraz with Tempranillo.

There are other excellent wineries in Western Australia. Howard Park started making great Cabernet blends in the Great Southern region and the Burch family produces its successful Madfish range in the Denmark region.

In the Frankland River region former sheep farmers Mervyn and Judy Lange produced their first Alkoomi wines in 1976. By the 1990s they were hitting their stride with some very impressive wines such as Blackbutt, a classic blend of the Cabernets, Malbec and Merlot. I was also impressed with their Frankland River Riesling. There are several other excellent Rieslings produced in the region.

Frankland Estate has earned a justified reputation for its excellent Cabernet blend and Olmo's Reward, a blend based on Cabernet Franc which is dedicated to the late Professor Olmo, a Californian grape breeder, who was so helpful in guiding regional viticulturalists toward the best sites for specific varieties.

McHenry, Hohnen Vintners was started up by David Hohnen of Cape Mentelle fame and his brother-in-law after the LVMH take-over in 2003. The company is effectively run the brother-in-law while Hohnen tends his Wiltshire sheep and Tamworth pigs. His daughter Freya is involved with her partner winemaker Ryan Walsh, working four good sized plots, one of which produces stunning Sauvignon Blanc. All the wines are well made with Cabernet Sauvignon being the pick of the reds.

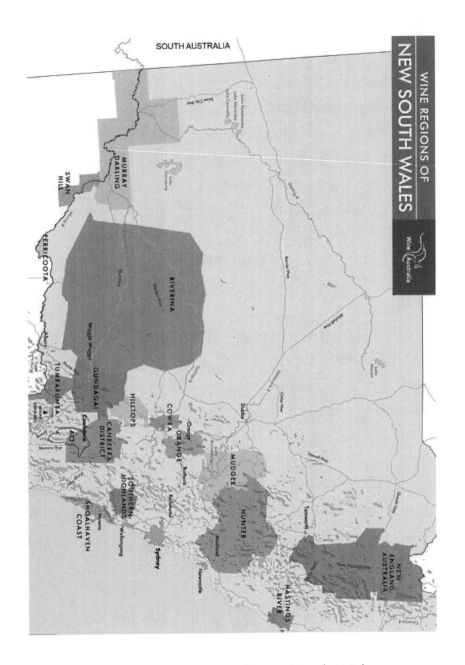

Wine Regions of New South Wales

NEW SOUTH WALES

HUNTER VALLEY

The Hunter Valley is the acknowledged birthplace of Australian wine. Yet its hot, humid summers and wet autumns are by no means ideal for a wine region. In fact, the highest rainfall of the year in the Hunter is often at harvest time. However, its proximity to Sydney (two hours away) made it popular with 'wannabe' wine growers who came up from the capital at weekend to tend their plots and have some fun.

Once wittily described as 'the triumph of proximity over suitability', the Hunter Valley has triumphed as a wine region because its vintners have made it an attractive region to visit and, more importantly, because they produces some of the world's finest and longest lived Semillon wines.

Like the Napa Valley in California, the Hunter draws wine tourists from all over the world. There is a wide choice of restaurants, guest houses, hotels, golf courses and other outdoor entertainments all designed to attract custom at hundreds of different Cellar Doors.

Dr Lindeman set the early pace in the 1830-1850 period followed by the fortified winemakers. In the 1920 the late and great Maurice O'Shea painstakingly created the Lovedale vineyard at Mount Pleasant to make some of the finest and longest lived Semillon and Shiraz wines ever produced in Australia. About the same time another legend, Dan '75 vintage' Tyrrell, headed the company which produced the first commercial Australian Chardonnay in 1971. It is also the region where Max Lake, surgeon and weekend winemaker, made superb Chardonnay and

Cabernet Sauvignon (against all odds for the region) at Lakes Folly: and it is also where the redoubtable Len Evans built himself a tin roofed, colonial style bungalow with wide verandas, to preside over the affairs of the Rothbury Estate that he founded and managed for its various investors for some time, and his Evans Wine Company.

Today the region is somewhat reduced in size from the 4,200 hectares planted at the height of the fortified wine trade. Now only 1600 hectares of the better vineyards remain in more experienced winemaking hands. It is true that some growers have gone into the cooler Upper Hunter where very fine Chardonnays and peppery, cool climate Shiraz wines are made.

The Hunter vineyards were made fruitful by the weathered volcanic soils of the Brokenback Mountains and the cloud cover that tempers the hottest sun. The almost sub-tropical conditions allow the Semillon to gain flavour ripeness at low alcohol levels. There is a very short ripening window of 30 days or so from veraison to harvest. According to old Hunter hands the secret is to pick early and ferment immediately in stainless steel to get stunning green-gold wines which are often ready to drink after six weeks showing zesty, grassy, citrus flavours. However, when yields are controlled, Semillon can also flourish and develop with age. Oak helps them acquire rich toasty flavours and they will last for years and years. The Hunter's climatic conditions suit the Semillon and there are still about 100 hectares of 100 year old vines.

MOUNT PLEASANT ESTATE

Mount Pleasant winery was created by the great Maurice O'Shea (1897-1956). Now owned by the McWilliams family (who for a long time gave O'Shea the financial backing that allowed him to concentrate on growing and vinifying his exceptional wines) Mount Pleasant makes classic Hunter Valley wines quite beautifully. The estate is run by Phil Ryan, only the third Mount Pleasant winemaker following Maurice O'Shea (left) and Brian Walsh (1956-78) Director of Wine at Yalumba. Between them, these three winemakers not only established a truly world class Semillon but have also garnered more gold medals for Lovedale than any other single vineyard Australian wine. It was a privilege and a memorable treat to be able to taste a selection of vintages from across the years in the company of Phil Ryan.

The story of Maurice O'Shea and Lovedale is reminder that there are no short cuts to the creation of great vineyards. Observation, vision, hope, persistence, patience, training, flair, talent, backbreaking work and more persistence, patience and purpose are required. Lovedale today is a tribute to a remarkable man and his belief that despite all

the difficulties, he could and would make great wine at Mount Pleasant.

O'Shea, born in Kerry, Ireland was trained at Montpellier in France where he stayed for a while after graduation to lecture in oenology. He developed a great skill for identifying quality wines in their early stages, and the know-how to develop them to their full potential. A master blender, he was brilliant at identifying flavours and selecting wines that would marry well together, and last a long time. Some of the wines he made more than fifty years ago are still drinking well.

Like all great winemakers he knew his terroir and realised that the sandy loam soils around Mount Pleasant were perfectly suited to Semillon despite the fact that other vintners considered the same soil to be so poor 'that rabbits would need to bring their own lunch box with them to survive.'

With the financial support of Keith McWilliam through the terrible years of the Depression, O'Shea patiently acquired the plots to create the Lovedale Estate, now a composite 30 hectare vineyard almost exclusively planted to Semillon.

Sadly O'Shea died prematurely of cancer and did not live to see the full development of the Australian fine wine trade that he did so much to foster. The McWilliams family has perpetuated his name with the annual Maurice O'Shea Award for the most outstanding vintner each year and it was entirely appropriate that the first winner of the award should be Max Schubert, the creator of Grange.

The sheer class of the Lovedale wines makes words superfluous. They are like works of art that you can actually savour. The occasion was made by having Phil Ryan guide us through the subtle variations of vintage of the superb Semillons and introduce us to the refined and rich Maurice O'Shea Hunter Shiraz wines. It was also good to taste the other wines in the McWilliams portfolio including a classy Evans & Tate Chardonnay from Western Australia, and a very polished Coonawarra Cabernet Sauvignon from the Laira vineyard.

McWILLIAMS

One of the largest wine companies in Australia, McWilliams was started by Samuel of the clan, who hailed from southern Ireland.

The company's roots are in Corowa village on the banks of the Murray River in the Upper Hunter. In 1917 they built a winery at Hanwood which was recently modernized to include state-of-the-art equipment allowing the winemaking team more opportunity to develop smaller parcels of special grapes.

In the 1950s Glen McWilliams shifted the emphasis from fortified to premium table wines and the company expanded dramatically and now has three winemaking centres. At Hilltops, which as the name suggests is high - 560 metres high – in New South Wales: at Coonawarra where it has one of the largest vineyard holdings: and in the Yarra valley Victoria where the vineyards at Lillydale are appropriately named Morning Light and Sunnyside. More recently McWilliams rescued Evans and Tate in Margaret River where rich generously fruity Chardonnays are made.

The company's decision to produce quality table wines has paid off. In 2010 McWilliams won 40 Trophies and 889 wine show medals. The Mount Pleasant Estate is their pride and joy, but all their wines, produced by the team of winemakers headed by Scott McWilliams, are of exemplary quality. Scott, the latest of the family line to take charge, was so keen to learn he started at the age of 14. 25 years later he is still learning how to ensure that the McWilliams name can be as trusted as ever.

TYRRELLS

Tyrrells is an even older company than McWilliams: the family celebrated its 150th birthday as a going concern in 2008. It has survived by constantly refining its winemaking techniques and producing wines that its customers appreciate. The company owns 360 hectares in four different locations- the Hunter Valley, the Limestone Coast, Heathcote Victoria and McLaren Vale.

Murray Tyrrell was one of the early enthusiasts for Chardonnay and admits to 'borrowing' some cuttings from his neighbour's vineyard and propagating them. Tyrells still produces Vat 47, a lean and elegant Chardonnay made without any malolactic fermentation.

However, the real attraction of our visit was the range of single vineyard Semillons that have made the company famous. We started by tasting current vintages before looking at the same styles with five years ageing. The mature wines develop colour with age and a rich, toasty flavour. We completed the Semillon tasting with a graceful 1998 Tyrells Vat 1, golden in colour, full of fresh citrus flavours.

Mark Richardson, the red winemaker, then showed us recent releases of the company's celebrated Shiraz wines. The 2005 Brokenback, produced from vines planted a the foot of the picturesque Brokenback Mountains (clearly visible from the winery) is a fine example of modern Hunter Shiraz, deep and dark with ripe fruits and a touch of spice but a degree or so lighter in alcohol than Barossa and McLaren Vale Shiraz. The superbly balanced 2005 single vineyard Stevens Shiraz was a wonderful reminder of just how very good Hunter Shiraz can be.

Bruce Tyrell is proud of his Shiraz and Chardonnay but claims with some pride that the Hunter produces the best Semillon in the world. 'We have other regions that can make similar claims for other varieties even if we have to substitute world for southern hemisphere, but this is the point that we should be getting across.'

I heartily concur.

TEMPUS TWO

The grey steel and black architecture of Tempus Two is quite different from that of most conventional wineries. But then it is meant to be because Liza McGuigan, the driving force of the business, has set out to attract a new audience to wine. Her aim is a contemporary, stylish, arresting and comfortable environment for her customers to enjoy tasting and selecting the wines they wish to purchase.

Fountains splash as you approach the Cellar Door which opens on to the stylish retail section and a plush modern reception area that would not be out of place in a five star hotel.

Liza, dressed from head to toe in black down to her brightly studded boots welcomed us with a big smile. Would the wines live up to the aesthetics?

We started with a clean and fruity entry-level Semillon-Sauvignon and followed it with sparkling Moscato made in the Asti style with 75g/L residual sugar and presented in an Italian designed bottle with a promotional promise to pour 'liquid sunshine.' Melange a Trois, a Viognier/Marsanne blend with a touch of Roussanne, had a pleasing floral nose and full flavoured palate.

The star of the show was Tempus Two Copper Zenith 2003 Semillon. Pristine citrus fruit flavours, elegance and style all combined to make this wine, kept four years before release, as something special. We also tasted a botrytised Semillon with 204 g/1 of residual sugar. Gorgeous golden colour, fresh apricot bouquet and opulent on the palate.

It is unlikely that, left to my own devices, I would have chosen to buy these wines for myself. But then I am not a youngish professional woman with my own sense of style. Liza McGuigan is an independent minded woman and a very astute marketer who knows precisely the market she wants to reach and makes and packages her wines accordingly.

She knows her facts too. 'Seventy percent of white wine is purchased by women who appreciate aromas and like fresh flavours.' The wines we tasted were made with these attributes in mind and packaged with panache. Some were even dressed with very distinctive stamped pewter labels. What I really admire about the whole Tempus Two set up is that

McGuigan has dared to be different and done it in style.

She took her inspiration from the classic European varieties but has treated them in a modern way with an appropriate Aussie twist. Her enormous energy and enthusiasm are catching. Her bold, imaginative, market-led approach works and is refreshingly different from that of traditional wineries. She has built brand awareness through association with popular music (bringing such superstars as Elton John to the winery for sponsored concerts) fashion, hairstyling, and home & garden events. She even promotes her wines through the Very Smelly Cheese Shop.

Tempus Two is a relevant, refreshing, exciting modern wine business which deserves to succeed. With all the glitz and the glamour it has not forgotten how to make good wines. The Tempus Two Copper Zenith Semillon 2004 has won a hatful of Show gold medals and the sweet honeyed tones of its Botrytised Semillon lingers on palate.

The red wines were also fruity, fresh, stylish and successful. Vine Vale Shiraz has just been selected by KLM to serve to its world

Business Class passengers. Tempus Two is part of the McGuigan Simeon Group, one of Australia's largest and most dynamic wineries which has excellent access to the best grapes around Australia. The red wines we tasted were mostly sourced from Coonawarra, Barossa and Langhorne Creek, as well as the Hunter's own Shiraz.

BROKENWOOD

Phil Kreiger welcomed us to this well-established winery opened in the 1970's by three young lawyers from Sydney, including James Halliday. Halliday, having worked in European wineries, took on the role of winemaker but when his law firm posted him to Melbourne he relinquished his interest. He later invested his time, energy and enthusiasm to starting up Coldstream Hills in the Yarra Valley.

The wines are now made by Kiwi winemaker PJ Charteris, who showed a good turn of speed around the cellar as he dipped into his precious casks of 2008's.It was particularly interesting to taste a Shiraz left to marinate on Viognier skins, a common practice in the Rhone, but one that you have to be there at the right time to enjoy. It certainly gives a lift to the Shiraz, both on the nose and the palate. The highlight of our visit was the 2005 Brokenwood Graveyard Shiraz, one of Australia's most outstanding wines at the beginning of its life in bottle. We were so impressed that we persuaded our driver to make a detour so that we could see the deep red loam soils from which the powerful yet elegant wine came. And to give thanks that the land that was actually designated for other purposes as its name suggests was turned to better use.

LEN EVANS OA OBE (1930-2006)

Len Evans, born and raised in East Anglia of Welsh parents, was an irrepressible enthusiast  for Australian wines who worked hard to advance their cause around the world.

Evans emigrated to New Zealand in 1953 and came to Australia two years later where, after a succession of jobs he became beverage manager at the newly opened Hilton Hotel in Sydney.

He was encouraged to learn about wine and such was his enthusiasm for the subject that he was later appointed National Promotions Executive for the Australian Wine and Brandy Corporation. Interestingly on his appointment he was directed to concentrate his efforts on fortified wines because 'there was no demand for table wines'.

Table wine was not generally appreciated in a beer drinking nation where the 'six o'clock swill'- an hour after-work to drink as many t beers as you could- was the way of life. Indeed when Evans once ordered a glass of wine in a bar he was asked: 'What are you, some kind of poof?'

In 1969 he opened his own wine bar and restaurant at Bulletin Place in Sydney and encouraged young Australians to try the very best wines from around the world. He publicised his wine bar by printing fliers advising potential customers that 'we have sold out of 1928 Pichon Longueville but we do have some of the 1934 vintage in stock.'

Like many Sydney-siders he took to the Hunter Valley with relish. With funds from a group of wealthy investors he created the 300 hectare Rothbury Estate (now part of Fosters' empire) where an ultra modern winery was built to make the fashionable wines of the day. Backed by his wealthy friend Peter Fox, he created the Evans Wine Company and conducted business from his nearby house which he named Loggerheads. Ever the wit, Evans delighted in telling people that they should visit because he and his wife Pat 'were often at Loggerheads'.

He made friends easily and helped young winemakers such as Brian Croser and James Halliday on their way. He became Chairman of Petaluma the company that Croser founded to produce ultra premium wines from 'distinguished sites'.

At about this time Sydney began to take over from Melbourne as the centre of the Australian wine trade and Evans was appointed Chairman of the Royal Sydney Show. His exceptional tasting skills were widely recognised and he was invited to judge wines at many Shows at home and abroad.

He became the international ambassador for Australian wines and was awarded the OBE and the Order of Australia for services to the Australian wine trade. Wine Spectator invited him to lead their Wine Experience in New York and he was voted Decanter Wine Personality of the Year in 1997.

A larger-than-life, inspirational character who was also a bon vivant and raconteur Evans was genuinely knowledgeable about his passions — wine and sculpture — and an enthusiastic fund raiser for the many different charities he supported.

He once remarked that wine could be divided into four categories: fancy, realistic, ordinary and very ordinary. 'We will do best if we stick to the realistic category,' he opined. It is fitting to end this notebook by recalling a great hearted man who really believed in the future of Australian wine.

CONCLUSION

Despite my thorough training in the wine trade I am not an authority on Australian (nor indeed any other wine) but I have been fortunate enough as a journalist to travel to many of the great wine regions of the world including Australia, and am glad to pass on what I have learned from meeting, and tasting with many of the leading Australian winemakers. Because this book is based on my experiences during my visits to Australia where I spent more time in some regions than others, its coverage is regretfully somewhat uneven and so I heartily recommend enthusiasts to invest in James Halliday's superb Wine Atlas of Australia.

I thank my good friend Paul Bouchard for persuading me to go in the early 1980s to see for myself the Australian's bold, innovative and refreshing approach to viniculture and winemaking. However, a rather more significant event was the official visit of the Masters of Wine in 1982. They gave their seal of approval to what they found, and it is not surprising that Australian wine sales took off soon after.

The phenomenal success of the basic Australian offering has given her vintners a platform from which to show what they can do with better rootstock and clonal material in more suitable sites. It may take a little while for this to get across to the general public but for those interested in fine wine there are plenty of very fine wines already available and most of them at reasonable prices.

As Australia seeks to reposition herself in the world wine market she can be encouraged by the success of the better of her leading brand owners as well as many of her 2300 regional vintners who, despite the current economic slow-down, have made a determined start to winning new customers.

As an enthusiast I tend to see the positive side of things, but I am aware of some of the difficulties that lie ahead as the oversupplied world wine market becomes more competitive.

However, Australia has shown that she has the wherewithal to maintain an attractive quality/price ratio and the drive to succeed in her new mission. And Wine Australia knows that future strategy needs to be amended. As a marketer I humbly suggest that more attention be paid to building brand equity rather than using promotional discounts that tend to reduce it.

Developing a strong consumer franchise for a wide range of wines is difficult at the best of times. But that is what is required. Bordeaux has done it over the centuries (and may need to fine-tune its approach) and the Rhone Valley more recently. In a fragmented market a strong Trade franchise will lead to a compelling consumer one if communication is focused. Wine Australia has done it before and there are already signs that she will do so again.

In the meantime the wines that will do the talking are getting better and better and I hope these notes will help you to understand why that is so.

Index

ACKNOWLEDGMENTS

As always I am eternally grateful to those who have encouraged my interest in wine, and in the case of Australia my friend Paul Bouchard, as well as all the winemakers who have been so generous with their time and their wines to taste.

I also acknowledge with sincere thanks the help from Australian Wine in supplementing my own photographs with their own including the cover picture taken by Matt Turner.

I am particularly grateful to my colleague and friend Peter F May who has edited these notes and given me very practical help in preparing them for publication.

I have used such excellent reference sources as *The Oxford Companion to Wine* (Edited by Jancis Robinson) *Vines, Grapes and Vines* by Jancis Robinson, Oz Clarke's *Wine Atlas*, *The Sotheby Wine Encyclopaedia* by Tom Stevenson, *The World Atlas of Wine* Sixth Edition by Jancis Robinson and Hugh

Johnson, Hugh Johnson's *Story of Wine*, James E Wilson's *Terroir*, Richard Smart's *Sunshine into Wine*, Michael Broadbent's *Vintage Wine* and James Halliday's *Australian Wine Atlas*.

If I have inadvertently overlooked any acknowledgements please let me know so that I can put the record straight.